# EVERYBODY WINS!

## 100 Social-Emotional Learning Games That Children Should Play

Dianne Schilling ◇ Terri Akin

INNERCHOICE Publishing

Illustrations by Roger Johnson

Cover Design by Dave Cowan

ISBN – 10: 1-56499-060-0
ISBN – 13: 978-1-56499-060-0

**INNERCHOICE Publishing**
15079 Oak Chase Court
Wellington, FL 33414

www.InnerchoicePublishing.com

# Contents

# INTRODUCTION

Scientific research into learning and the human brain is currently exploding with discoveries about how humans learn best. It's now widely recognized that neuroplasticity (the ability of the human brain to grow, learn, and change throughout life) can, and should be, positively enhanced by schooling. Compelling evidence suggests that if educators understand how the brain learns and implement the correct skill-building educational experiences, all students can experience success.

This current research explosion has made it apparent that physical movement is critical to learning. Voluntary large motor activities such as games, team sports, dance, and running raise the good brain chemicals needed for learning, focus, thinking and memory access, and also help to reduce stress. Since chronic, acute stress negatively impacts learning and behavior, providing regular physical activity becomes a natural de-stressor and an important part of any school day. Research suggests that students benefit from 30 to 60 minutes per day of movement and organized physical activity.

Pro-social games of all kinds offer additional important ways to purposefully promote social and emotional learning. The natural desire of children to play together and have fun makes games an ideal delivery system for teaching important life skills. Through the structure, rules, and social interaction of games, children learn to share and take turns. They practice self-control and the effective management of negative emotions. They learn that motivation and persistence pay off. Games teach children the benefits of interacting with others in fair, just, and respectful ways, and help develop the critical life skills of collaboration and teamwork.

These important social and emotional skills are not innate talents, but learned abilities. The acquisition of social-emotional skills is facilitated by the structure and rules of games, by peer interaction, and also by adults modeling these behaviors and helping students to make appropriate learning connections.

*Everybody Wins!* is an eclectic collection of classic and "new" games. Included are familiar games like "Hide and Seek," "Hopscotch," and "Hang Man," which may belong to your own childhood repertoire, their rules partially eclipsed by time. We've included step-by-step procedures so that you can renew your acquaintance with these classic games and pass them on intact to your students. Also included are playful inventions belonging to the "new games" generation, which emphasize individual challenge, along with group creativity, cooperation, and caring.

We have attempted to select games that require a variety of skills. Many develop traditional sports skills such as strength, speed, coordination, and quick reflexes. Others emphasize interpersonal and interactive skills. Still others promote the use of brain power, strategic thinking, humor, and acting ability. All of the games encourage inclusion, cooperation, and full participation.

## Play With A Purpose

Since one of the primary ways social and emotional skills are developed in children is through play, in a school setting it should be play with a purpose. Guided lessons that allow children to be playfully and joyfully involved provide them opportunities to actively explore, manipulate and interact with their environment and with others. A lot of work and skill building is occurring when children play — they are learning to solve problems, make decisions, take turns, work in teams, (sometimes leading and sometimes following), express their opinions and ideas, and listen to others. It's through this adult-guided "play" that children can investigate, discover, take risks and create — all adding to their understanding of themselves, others and the world around them. The fun-filled, hands-on activities provided in *Everybody Wins!* give educators concrete lessons so that children can enjoy play with a purpose.

## Cooperation and Competition

Over the years, you've probably been exposed to considerable debate concerning the concepts of win-win, win-lose, and lose-lose. Our culture consistently places the highest value on winning, often at any cost. Sporting events of all kinds glorify winning and denigrate losing, and this attitude is frequently passed on in the activities that we organize for children. We think this practice is unfortunate and wish to emphasize from the start that full participation, not winning, is the goal of this book.

We're not suggesting that competition be completely eliminated from play. This is neither possible nor desirable. Some students are inherently more competitive than others and no one should deny those students the right to be themselves. However, through basic ground rules, the general tone you establish, and the way each game is monitored, the influence of overly competitive players can be minimized, while the values of cooperation and participation are maximized.

Competitive elements exist in many games. In tag games, players compete to run fastest (or smartest) from "It." In ball games, they compete to be strongest, speediest, or most agile. However, if winning is allowed to become the most important focus of a game, anyone who is less able, looks foolish, or makes a mistake loses value as a player. And to the extent that winning compromises the spirit of inclusion and cooperation or damages the self-esteem of even a single player, *everybody* loses.

So, instead of focusing on the outcome of a game, we urge you to emphasize participation, inclusion, and effort. In so doing, you'll *de-emphasize* the importance of the outcome and, thus, of winning. The ultimate outcome of *Everybody Wins!* is a positive climate in which *all* those who participate win.

**Ground Rules That Promote Inclusion**

Your class is a *single team* that frequently subdivides to play games and work on various academic projects. To help coalesce the entire team and establish a win-win spirit in play, we suggest that you ask your students to help you establish some basic ground rules that apply to all games. You might have small groups of students brainstorm suggested rules. After combining ideas and discussing a wide range of possibilities, get the entire class to agree on a final list, which might look something like this:

- Everyone gets to play.
- No one is forced to play.
- Listen to the leader.
- Rule changes must have the agreement of all players.
- Think strategy and practice teamwork.
- No criticism, teasing, or put downs.
- No rough play or fighting.

Once your students have helped establish the ground rules for play, make all of them responsible for enforcing the rules. Empower players by imbuing them with a spirit of "player/referee."

Ground rules can prove particularly helpful when dealing with more aggressive players. Natural athletes, for example, tend to be more competitive. Games are a perfect place for them to obtain recognition. By helping to establish and enforce ground rules, talented athletes can earn recognition while helping the entire group succeed. The same process helps timid players assume greater responsibility and feel more secure.

## Pre-game Presentations and Polling

The way you present a game greatly affects the way it is played. Whether you're explaining a game to three students or the entire class, the same advice applies: Explain the game's procedure and rules as clearly and simply as possible, and do it in a style that encourages participation, playfulness, and fun.

Because the brain needs time to process input and determine what action to take, it's best to give directions one at a time. Allow young brains plenty of processing time.

Begin by describing the game in a general way. Start with its name and explain its objective, mentioning any familiar games (or categories of games) that it resembles. Throughout your description, use empowering, inviting, and inclusive language. "Let's give this a try," instead of "You must..." Share *your* enthusiasm, *your* excitement, and *your* concerns with players.

If possible, combine your description with a demonstration. Give your demonstration a personal style, and model the type of play you want to encourage. How you model a particular role, such as the "Curator" in "Wax Museum," will determine how the players view that role, at least initially. Have everyone practice new or difficult moves before the game starts. Give students an opportunity to ask questions and express their own concerns. And, finally, remind students of the basic ground rules.

When you mention the word *game*, you may notice that natural athletes immediately become enthusiastic and enlivened, while less physically inclined players begin to withdraw. If this is the case in your group, consider giving students an opportunity to express their feelings before the game begins. For example, ask the students to rate their enthusiasm on a scale of 1 to 10. Or simply go around the group and ask how everyone is feeling. Another possibility is to play one of the communication or get-acquainted games as a warm up.

## Choosing Teams and Sides

Anyone who recalls the trauma of being the last person chosen for a team won't knowingly visit that same humiliation on his or her students. Here are a few noncompetitive methods for forming teams:

- Have boys form one line and girls another. Direct the players in both lines to count off by fours. Then create different combinations of players, depending on the number of teams required for the game. For example, announce that the 1's and 3's (both boys and girls) will form one team and the 2's and 4's another. Or have the 4's from the boys' line join the 1's from the girls' line. The purpose of counting by four's instead of the traditional two's is to prevent students from mastering the method and arranging themselves in line with the intent of loading a team. The purpose of segregating boys from girls initially is to achieve gender balance on the final teams.

- Write the names of animals on slips of paper and have every student draw a slip from a box . The number of teams required determines the number of different animals represented in the box. For example, if you need four teams, include an equal number of slips labeled *cat*, *dog*, *cow*, and *owl*. Then, without revealing the animal they drew, have the players "find" each other with meows, barks, moos, and hoots.

- Have every student choose a partner. This process generally pairs students of equal athletic ability. Then, in order to redistribute players into evenly-matched teams, break up those

6

pairs so that one partner ends up on Team A and the other partner on Team B. Use some unusual or amusing criterion to split the pairs. For example, have the student in each pair who has the longest hair join one team and the remaining student join the second team. Alternative criteria might be "shortest nails," "lightest color socks," "heaviest eyebrows," "most freckles," etc.

- Divide the group according to food preferences, such as vanilla vs. chocolate, or sweet vs. dill pickles. Use clothing, such as white and colored socks, or family relationships (first child, second child, middle child, etc.) Once you have divided the group, recombine the smaller groups till you achieve the required number and size of teams.

- As much as possible, work to strengthen positive social interaction among students. Create pre-planned groupings, teams, and buddy systems that result in positive student interaction. Social conditions influence the brain in multiple ways. Students who feel left out and "socially defeated" are found to have fewer brain cells. Positive student-to-student relationships matter. Use your authority to help create pro-social teams and groups.

## During Play

As a leader, be an alert observer, ready to adapt any game to the needs of your students. If a game involves running and slow runners appear frustrated, change the pace for a while, requiring toe-to-heel movements that put all players on a more equal footing. If the object of the game proves too difficult to achieve, take a time out and ask the players to help you invent a simpler objective for the game. On the other hand, if you observe signs of boredom, ask the players to think of ways to increase the level of challenge.

7

Always involve the players in the process of adapting a game. Ask, "How can we make the game more challenging?" or "How can we change the rules so that everyone has a chance to be 'It'?"

If the game you are playing requires that players be eliminated from play, try to re-involve them as quickly as possible. In some cases, players can become referees; in others they might be able to organize a separate game. In still others, instead of being permanently "out," they can be invited to rejoin the game after a single round.

If a player gets too rough, it should be everyone's responsibility to remind that player of the basic ground rules established by the group. With every person acting as a player/referee, most problems of this nature will be solved quickly; however, don't hesitate to impose an "out" on an overly rough player for a round or two.

## Post-game Discussions

Participation doesn't necessarily end when a game is over. Once back in class, prolong the involvement of players by giving them an opportunity to talk about the particular game experience. One of the best ways to accomplish this is by facilitating a brief class discussion. Stimulate thinking, creativity, and self and social awareness by asking open-ended questions such as these:

- What did you like best about this game?
- How did you feel while playing the game?
- What would you change about the game and why?
- What ideas does this game give you for creating a new game?
- When playing games, what do you say to encourage yourself?
- What can you say to your teammates to encourage them?
- When did you notice yourself working the hardest?

- Is it always important to win the game? Explain your answer.
- What kinds of problems did you encounter as a team, and how did you resolve them?
- When playing a game, is it important to think of your whole team or just yourself? Explain your answer.
- What have you learned about teamwork from this game?

Another possibility is to have the players form groups of six to eight, and share their thoughts and feelings in response to a specific topic, such as "What I Liked Best About "Peanut Butter and Jelly'" or "How I Was a Winner in 'Hug Tag.'"

Games are an excellent vehicle for developing not just physical skills, but cognitive and social-emotional learning as well. Games can help instill a spirit of inclusion and cooperation in your group that will spill over to the rest of the school day. After playing games, children return to class and academic study refreshed and ready to learn.

# *ACTION GAMES*

To encourage maximum participation in active games, here are
several classics that have proven their durability and popularity
through many generations of enthusiastic use.  Use them to help
players develop a flair for game strategy, stimulate originality and a
sense of humor, and share in fun of fast interaction.

# 1

# *Hide-and-Seek*

**Objective:**
To hide, then rush to get to "home" before "It;" to spy players, identify them by name, and reach "home" before they do.

**Players:**
3 or more

**Ages:**
6 and up

**Materials:**
none

**Setting:**
outdoors

**Directions:**
One person volunteers, or is selected, to be "It." All players start out at a tree, lamppost, or other large object, called "home." "It" turns around, closes his eyes, leans against home with his head on his arms, and counts to 100. The other players run and hide. When "It" reaches 100, he calls out, "Ready or not, here I come!" He then opens his eyes, turns around, and begins searching for the other players. When he sees a player, he shouts, "I spy (name of person)," at which time both he and the other player race for home. If the player touches home first, she yells, "Home free!" "It" then continues his search for other players. If "It" reaches home first, he calls out, "Ollie, Ollie, in free!" and all the other players return home for a new game in which the person who lost the race home becomes "It."

# 2

# *Quack, Quack*

**Objective:**

To guess the identity of other players by the sound of their voices.

**Players:**

8 or more

**Ages:**

6 and up

**Materials:**

blindfold and broomstick

**Setting:**

outdoors or a large room

**Directions:**

One player is chosen to be blindfolded and to hold the broomstick. The rest of the players form a circle and begin to walk around her. When the blindfolded player taps the broomstick on the ground three times, the players must stop walking. Then she points the broomstick toward the circle, and the player closest to spot at which she is pointing must call out, "Quack, quack." If she guesses who the person is on the first guess, she trades places with that player, who is blindfolded and given the broomstick. If she guesses incorrectly, everyone walks around her again until she taps, points, and makes a second guess as to who said, "Quack, quack."

# 3

# *Jan-Kem-Po*

**Objective:**
To show the dominant sign between two of three possible hand signs.

**Players:**
2 or more

**Ages:**
7 and up

**Materials:**
none

**Setting:**
indoors or outdoors

**Directions:**
This game is played in Japan and utilizes the same hand signs as the game, "Rock, Scissors, Paper." Players demonstrate the "rock" sign by making a fist with one hand; "scissors" is done by holding out the index and middle fingers in a V shape; "paper" is done by holding the hand out flat with fingers spread. Dominance among the signs is as follows: "rock" breaks scissors; "scissors" cut paper; and "paper" covers rock.

Two players face each other. Both players rub one forearm with the closed fist of the other arm three times and call, "Jan-Kem-Po." When "Po" is called, each player thrusts his or her hand forward, making one of the three hand signs and hoping to beat the sign of the other player. Remember: rocks beats scissors, scissors beat paper, and paper beats rock. The game can also be played by a group of players. The players form a circle with one person standing in the middle. Everyone calls "Jan-Kem-Po" and holds the hand positions out at the same time. Any player who beats the center player 3 times becomes the center player for the next round.

# Leapfrog

**Objective:**

To leap over the backs of other players and to crouch down while others leap over you.

**Players:**

3 or more

**Ages:**

6 and up

**Materials:**

**Setting:**

an outdoor grassy area or spacious indoor area with tumbling mats

**Directions:**

Players line up in a row, facing the same direction. The first player in line bends over, hands braced on her knees, or squats down with hands touching the ground between her legs. The second player places his hands on the first player's back, spreads his legs wide, jumps over the first player, and assumes the same squatting position. The third player leaps over the first two, the fourth leaps over the first three, and so on to the last player in line. When that person has jumped over all the other players, the first person gets up and leaps over everyone, continuing the game until a barrier or preset distance is reached. Once the first person has had her chance to leap over everyone, the players can make the line move faster by agreeing that as soon as a player leaps over two people, the next player gets up and starts leaping, too. In this way, more than one person is moving down the line at once.

# 5

# *The Jungle Game*

**Objective:**

To pantomime any part of a specified jungle scene on command.

**Players:**

12 or more

**Age:**

8 and up

**Materials:**

**Setting:**

an open space outdoors or indoors

**Directions:**

All jungle scenes in this game are created by groups of three players. Therefore, players practice the scenes in three's as well. A "palm tree" is made when the center person stands straight with arms raised to the sky. The players on either side stand up against the center and lean over with their arms arching. "Monkeys" are made in a family of three: the first player covers his eyes to represent, "See no evil;" the middle player covers her ears to pantomime, "Hear no evil;" and the third player poses as, "Speak no evil," by covering his mouth. The "elephant" is created by having the middle person stand with arms outstretched and hands clasped to form a "trunk." The players on either side become the "ears" by forming large circles with their arms and placing them against the elephant's head. All players practice all parts of the three jungle scenes.

The game begins when players form a circle and one stands in the middle, becoming the "spinner." The "spinner" turns around holding one arm straight out and pointing a finger. When she stops spinning, she calls out one of the jungle scenes, "palm tree," "monkeys," or "elephant." The person to whom she is pointing becomes the center of the specified jungle scene and the players on either side join in to complete the scene. Any player who fumbles over his or her part in the scene changes places with the "spinner." If all three players create the scene without hesitation or mistakes, the "spinner" takes another turn.

# 6

# *Red Rover*

**Objective:**
To break through a line of linked hands, or to prevent someone from breaking through your line of linked hands.

**Players:**
8 or more

**Ages:**
8 and up

**Materials:**
none

**Setting:**
a large grassy area outdoors

**Directions:**
This game originated in Scotland during the late 1800's as "Jockey Rover" and is definitely not for the delicate. Players divide into two equal teams and each team selects a leader. The teams form lines about 15 to 20 feet apart, holding hands and facing each other. One leader starts the game by delivering a challenge to a player on the other team. She calls out, "Red Rover, Red Rover, we dare (person's name) to come over." The person on the opposite team who is named drops hands with his teammates and charges to the other line, trying to break through any two linked hands. If he breaks a link, he gets to take back to his team the two players whose hands were unlinked. If he cannot break through, he remains with the other team as a new member. Leaders alternately call a player from the other team by chanting the rhyme. The game ends when one team is reduced to a single player, which is very difficult. Usually the numbers are shifted and rebalanced throughout the game.

# 7

# *Wax Museum*

**Objective:**
To tag other players and "form" them into creative "sculptures;" to avoid being tagged and to "rescue" other players who have been caught and sculpted.

**Players:**
6 or more

**Ages:**
6 and up

**Materials:**
none

**Setting:**
outdoors in an open area

**Directions:**
One player is selected to be the "Curator" of the "Wax Museum." The Curator chases the other players and attempts to tag them. The other players, of course, try to avoid being tagged by dodging and running away from the Curator. When the Curator tags a player, that player must freeze, as in a game of "Freeze Tag." However, once the player is frozen, the Curator twists and shapes the arms, legs, and body of the frozen player into a funny, grotesque, or stately "wax" sculpture in her museum. The wax sculpture must remain in the sculpted position until two other players "bring him back to life" by joining hands in a circle around him. However, these players do so at risk of being frozen and sculpted by the Curator, who is always searching for new sculptures for her museum. The game ends when the Curator has turned all remaining players into wax sculptures, thus completing her museum. If the group is large, two Curators may be chosen to quicken the pace of the game.

# *Jackstones*

**Objective:**

To pick up one or more stones while a ball is in the air and catch the ball after one bounce.

**Players:**

2 or more, small groups of 4 or less

**Ages:**

7 and up

**Materials:**

5 to 10 jacks (or stones) and one ball per pair or small group

**Setting:**

anywhere there is a flat surface

**Directions:**

Originally called "Jackstones," jacks were once small pebbles which were picked up from the ground as one pebble was tossed into the air. Now Jacks is commonly played with a small rubber ball. In both versions, a player plays until he or she makes a mistake. Then the turn goes to the next player, and the next, and so on back to the original player. There are several kinds of Jacks games. Here are a few:

In **"Baby Jacks,"** a player scatters the jacks on a flat surface. He then tosses the ball up with one hand, picks up one jack with the same hand, and catches the ball after one bounce using the same hand. He transfers the jack to the other hand and tries for the next jack in the same way. He continues until he makes a mistake or retrieves all of the jacks. In **"Pigs in the Pen,"** the player scatters the jacks, and then cups her non-throwing hand over the playing surface. She tosses the ball up, lifts the thumb of the cupped hand, and, with her throwing hand, slides a jack inside the "pen" before catching the ball. She continues this until all of the "pigs" are in the "pen." **"Eggs in the Basket"** is played by tossing the jacks and picking them up one-by-one as the ball is tossed, each time transferring them to the non-throwing hand until all "eggs" are in the "basket." In **"Sheep Over the Fence,"** the player places his non-throwing hand on its side, with the fingers stacked. During each toss of the ball, he takes a jack and places it on the palm side of the fence, continuing until all "sheep" are "over the fence." In **"Crack the Eggs,"** the player tosses the ball, picks up a jack, and taps the jack on the playing surface before catching the ball. Each jack is transferred to the non-throwing hand before "cracking" the next "egg." **"Two's, Three's and Four's..."** is played when players have mastered retrieving one jack at a time in the various games. After "one's" a player tries for "two's," "three's," "four's," and so on until she finally picks up all of the scattered jacks on one toss of the ball.

# 9

# *Jumprope*

**Objective:**
To jump over a rope as it is turned while reciting various rhymes.

**Players:**
1 or more

**Ages:**
6 and up

**Materials:**
short ropes for solo jumpers; a long rope for each group of 6 to 8

**Directions:**
A single person holds a rope in both hands and turns it over his head, jumping over it in single or double jumps when it touches the ground. Rhymes may be recited while jumping like, "My mother is a butcher, My father cuts the meat, And I'm a little hot dog, Just running 'round the street," or "I love coffee, I love tea, I love the boys (or girls), And the boys (or girls) love me." A single player can also travel (move forward) while jumping. A "jumping-rope race" can be played between two or more single jumpers running forward while they jump.

Groups can play jumprope games in which players jump in and out of the rope or do stunts while jumping. Two players volunteer to turn the rope while others take turns jumping. One chant starts with the rope holders swaying the rope back and forth while the jumper jumps and chants, "Blue bells, cockle shells, Eevy, ivy, over" On "over," the rope holders turn the rope over while the jumper recites a new chant. Another chant involves several jumpers who enter at different cues: "Mother, Mother, I am sick; Call for the doctor, quick, quick, quick; In comes the doctor (a new jumper jumps

22

in); In comes the nurse (another jumper joins them); In comes the lady with the alligator purse (a third player jumps in); Out goes the doctor (the one who entered as the doctor jumps out); Out goes the nurse (the nurse jumps out); Out goes the lady with the alligator purse (the third player leaves). Still another chant starts with three or four jumpers. They chant, "Apples, peaches, pears, and plums; Tell me when your birthday comes." Then they call out the months of the year in order, and each player jumps out on his or her birthday. During another chant, a jumper performs these tricks as spoken: "Teddy bear, Teddy bear, Turn around (jumper turns around); Teddy Bear, Teddy Bear, Touch the ground (jumper touches the ground); Teddy Bear, Teddy Bear, Show your shoes (jumper kicks out one foot at a time); Teddy Bear, Teddy Bear, Read the news (jumper holds hands up as if reading a newspaper)." There are hundreds of rhymes and chants from all over the world and jump-ropers make up new ones daily.

# 10

# *Fox and Chickens*

**Objective:**
To tag the last person in a line if you are the "fox;" to protect your chicks if your are the "hen;" to escape from being tagged if you are a "chick."

**Players:**
8 or more

**Ages:**
5 and up

**Materials:**
none

**Setting:**
an open area outdoors

**Directions:**
One player is selected to be the "fox." The rest line up behind one another with hands on the shoulders of the person in front. The player at the head of the line is the "hen" and those behind him are the "chicks." The game begins when the hen and chicks start marching slowly toward the crouching fox, reciting the following chant, "Chickany, chickany, crany crow; I went to the well to wash my toe; When I came back a chicken was dead." At that point the line should stop in front of the fox. The hen asks the fox, "What time is it, mean old fox?" The fox counts the chicks and answers, "Eight o'clock (or whatever number matches the count of chicks), for I see eight chicks." Next the hen asks, "What are you doing, mean old fox?" The fox replies, "Picking up sticks." The conversation continues. Hen: "What for?" Fox: "To make a fire." Hen: "What do you want a fire for?" Fox: "To cook a chicken."

Hen: "Where will you get it?" Fox: "I'll catch one of yours!" As the fox speaks that line, she springs up and begins chasing the line of chicks, trying to tag the last one. The chicken flaps its wings and leads the line of chicks out of the way of the fox. When the fox tags the last chick in line, she becomes the hen and the chick that was tagged becomes the fox. The line rotates in that way so that all players get to be the hen, fox, and last chick. The game can be varied so that the fox and hen keep their positions, and the fox captures a new chick each round and puts it into his "den" until all chicks have been taken captive.

# *BALL GAMES*

The ball is probably the simplest and most readily available piece of equipment and lends itself to the greatest variety of games, whether for a single player or a group. Give a ball to any two or more students and, even if they speak different languages, they are bound to achieve a degree of understanding.

The seven games in this section require a minimum of four or more players. Some of the games are played with a single ball, others call for multiple balls. The games have been chosen to develop coordination and skill in bouncing, throwing, and other aspects of ball handling; to provide practice in the use of gross motor skills; and to stimulate social interaction.

# 11

# *Spud*

**Objective:**

To avoid being labeled with the letters S-P-U-D by hitting another player with the ball; to avoid being hit by the ball.

**Players:**

4 or more

**Ages:**

7 and up

**Materials:**

a large bouncing ball

**Setting:**

grassy area or hardtop outdoors

**Directions:**

One player is chosen to hold the ball while the other players gather around her. She tosses the ball high into the air and calls out the name of another player who must catch the ball. In the meantime, all other players, including the ball tosser, run away from the ball as fast as they can. As soon as the person named catches the ball, he calls out, "Spud," and the players freeze in their tracks. The player with the ball looks around to find the closest player and takes four giant steps toward that player, spelling out S-P-U-D as the steps are taken. He then tries to hit that person with the ball. If the player is hit with the ball, she is given the letter "S." If the ball tosser misses the victim, he gets the letter "S." Whoever receives the letter becomes the ball tosser for the next round. Players who accumulate all four letters, S-P-U-D, are out.

# 12

# *Peanut Butter and Jelly*

**Objective:**

To pass two balls around a circle, starting first one and then the other, to see if the second can catch up with the first.

**Players:**

8 or more

**Ages:**

7 and up

**Materials:**

two rubber balls or two inflatable beach balls

**Setting:**

outdoor or a spacious indoor area

**Directions:**

Players stand in a circle and someone begins to pass around one of the balls. This is the Peanut Butter ball. Everyone must pass the ball with both hands as fast as possible. When the ball is about halfway around the circle, the person who started passing the first ball begins passing the second one in the same direction. Players pass both balls as rapidly as possible without dropping them. The object is to observe how long it takes for the second ball to catch up with the first. The player who ends up catching both balls calls out, "Peanut Butter and Jelly!" and that ends the game. The game can be varied so that the player who ends up with both the Peanut Butter and Jelly gets to start the next game.

# 13

# *Prisoner Rollball*

**Objective:**

To roll a ball so that it touches an opponent while avoiding being hit
by a ball rolled by an opponent.

**Players:**

8 or more

**Ages:**

8 and up

**Materials:**

3 to 6 medium-sized rubber balls

**Setting:**

a playground with a painted 25-yard square divided by a center line,
or enough cones to mark off a 25-yard square with a center line
dividing it (sizes may be approximated) .

**Directions:**

Players divide into two teams.  If teams consist of fewer than 5
players each, use only two balls.  Larger teams may start with two
balls, increasing to three if faster play is desired.  Each team must
stay inside its half of the large square playing field while playing the
game.  The only exception to this rule applies to "prisoners," who
stand behind the end line of the opposing team.  One person from
each team volunteers to start off as a prisoner to retrieve balls that
pass beyond the end line.

The game begins when a ball is rolled from each team toward a
player on the opposite team with the intent of hitting that player
below the knees.  Any other body part touched by the ball does not
count as a "hit."  Players may catch or dodge the rolling balls.  Any

balls caught are immediately rolled back toward the opposing team. Team members who are hit become prisoners and stand behind the end line of the opposing team. Prisoners must catch balls that roll over the end line and may roll these balls back at their opponents. This creates a game where balls are being rolled in both directions. If a prisoner gets hit, that prisoner is freed and may return to his or her team's side of the field. Players may not step over the end line or the middle line to catch or roll the ball. The game ends when all players of one team are in prison.

# 14

# *Crazy Pass*

**Objective:**

To pass balls around a circle in different directions and in different ways.

**Players:**

8 or more

**Ages:**

6 and up

**Materials:**

2 or more rubber balls or inflatable beach balls

**Setting:**

an open area outdoors or indoors

**Directions:**

Players stand in a circle and begin passing a ball around in any manner they choose. The ball can be passed overhead, under the legs, behind the body, one-handed, or in any creative way a player can invent. After the first ball gets started, players begin passing a second ball in the opposite direction. At any point, the leader may call, "Change," signaling that players who are holding the balls must pass them in the opposite direction. Vary the game by having players give each ball a name, which must then be called out each time that ball is touched. For example, one ball might be named "Bruno" and the other, "Slash." The players must say the correct name each time a ball is passed. More fun and confusion can be generated by entering additional balls into play. The game ends when the players are laughing too hard to play or are so confused by the directions and names that balls begin to drop.

# 15

# *Tunnel Kickball*

**Objective:**

To score as many points as possible for one's team by kicking a rolled ball and running the bases; to prevent the kicker from scoring points by, as quickly as possible, retrieving the ball and passing it through a tunnel made up of all players in the field.

**Players:**

8 or more

**Ages:**

8 and up

**Materials:**

soccer ball or other sturdy kick ball; pencils and paper or scorecard

**Setting:**

A baseball diamond or grassy area with 4 bases

**Directions:**

Players divide into two equal teams. One team starts in the field and the other team is "up." The players in the field scatter to catch the ball. A pitcher begins the game by rolling the ball to the first kicker on the opposite team. After that kicker kicks the ball, he runs around the bases, scoring a point for each base reached before he hears the word, "Freeze!" All players of the fielding team run to where the ball has been kicked and line up behind the person who catches the ball. With their legs spread apart, the team passes the ball under each pair of legs from the first to the last player in line. When the last person gets the ball, she calls out, "Freeze," which stops the runner from scoring any more points. Points are recorded on paper, in the dirt, or on a score card. After each member of the team that is "up" has kicked, the teams switch sides. There are no strikes or outs, only "freezes," which limit the number of points scored by the other team. The game can be played through as many innings as the players choose.

# 16

# *Bounce-VolleyBall*

**Objective:**
To hit a ball over the net after it has bounced once on the ground.

**Players:**
8 or more

**Ages:**
8 and up

**Materials:**
volleyball net; volleyball or medium-sized rubber ball

**Setting:**
volleyball court

**Directions:**
Players divide into two teams. Each team spreads out on one side of the net. Players may rotate and take turns serving as in regular volleyball. The serve changes sides each time a team fails to return the ball.

The ball is served by a player on one side. Any teammate may help the server hit the ball over the net. After the ball flies over the net, it must bounce once on the ground before being hit by a player on the other side. Teammates may assist by hitting the ball as many times as necessary to return the ball over the net, *without its hitting the ground again.* However, the game is non-competitive and no points are scored when a team misses. The game is a cooperative effort to keep track of how many times the ball is volleyed over the net, and to break each successive new record.

# 17

# *Spaceball*

**Objective:**
To hit someone by rolling a ball or to
avoid being hit by a rolling ball.

**Players:**
10 or more

**Ages:**
8 and up

**Materials:**
4 to 8 medium-sized rubber balls

**Setting:**
A playground or blacktop with a small prepainted circle (about 6 feet in
diameter) inside a larger prepainted circle (about 20 feet in diameter).

**Directions:**
Two players are selected to be the "spaceships" inside the smaller
circle. Two other players are selected to be "enemy space stations"
outside the larger circle. The rest of the players divide into pairs,
hold hands, and move around the inside of the large circle as
"asteroids." The two spaceships start with two to four balls each,
and roll these balls, one at a time, toward the moving asteroids, who
try to dodge the balls. If any partner is hit by a rolled ball below the
knee, the asteroid "explodes" and leaves the asteroid belt to join the
enemy space stations outside the large circle. The task of the enemy
space stations is to roll the retrieved balls toward the spaceships in
the smaller circle, hitting them below the knee. The spaceships try
to catch the rolled balls instead of being hit. If a spaceship is hit,
he or she must leave the small circle and join the enemy outside the
large circle. Asteroids mistakenly hit by the enemy space stations
do not explode. The game ends when either no asteroids are left in
the large circle or no spaceships are left in the small circle.

# 18

# *Over Under*

**Objective:**

To pass a ball along a line alternating over a head, under a pair of legs, and so on.

**Players:**

12 or more

**Ages:**

6 and up

**Materials:**

medium-sized rubber balls

**Setting:**

an open space, outdoors or indoors

**Directions:**

This game can be played in teams as a relay or in a single long line, just for fun. Players stand in line facing forward. The first player in line holds a ball and at "Go," passes the ball over her head to the second player in line. The second player takes the ball and passes it under his legs to the third player. The third player passes it overhead, and each remaining player alternates passing under, over, under, etc. When the last person gets the ball, she runs to the front of the line and starts the process again. The game continues until every player has had a turn at the head of the line and the original first player is back in front.

Vary the game by using more than one ball, especially if your group is large. The first player starts the first ball overhead. Then when that ball is four or five players down the line, he passes the second ball under his legs. If the line is more than 15 players long, he can start a third ball. Each time a player receives a ball one way (for example, over), she must pass it the alternate way (under). The end player always runs to the front and starts passing the ball again, in the alternate way (over or under). The game ends when the players are totally confused or laughing so hard that they can no longer pass the balls.

# BRAIN GAMES

Games that challenge the mind are perfect for inclement weather, for warming up (or waking up) a group prior to introducing a new assignment, or as exercise breaks for the brain. Make them a regular part of your mental workout program!

The games in this section are intended to stretch the mind, encouraging players to think creatively and divergently to solve problems. Use them to generate new ideas, and to stimulate originality, strategic thinking, and memory.

# 19

# *Memory*

**Objective:**
To remember items in a box, details of a picture, or objects in a room.

**Players:**
2 or more

**Ages:**
5 and up

**Materials:**
small objects in a shoe box; a picture with many details, or a furnished room

**Setting:**
indoors or outdoors

**Directions:**
One player fills a shoe box full of small objects such as a flashlight, safety pin, curler, fork, matches, pen, pencil, eraser, crayon, key chain, ring, watch, nail file, scissors, small toy, and so on. All other players are given one minute to examine the contents of the box. After a minute, the lid is placed on the box and players take turns trying to list as many of the objects as they can remember. The person who remembers the most is the winner. Any wrong answers are subtracted from the total of right ones. Each player can bring his or her own box full of objects to create additional games. Detailed pictures can be used instead of boxes of tangible objects. A furnished room is another possibility. Players are given one minute to look around the room, then leave the room and test their memory by each making a list of the room's furnishings. Or the players may brainstorm a single list to see if the whole group can remember every detail.

# 20

# *I Spy*

**Objective:**

To try to guess an object in a room by asking "yes" or "no" questions about the description of the object.

**Players:**

8 or more

**Ages:**

8 and up

**Materials:**

**Setting:**

a room filled with furniture and other objects

**Directions:**

One player is chosen to be the "spy." The spy looks around the room and selects a secret object. He then says, "I spy something in this room." The other players become "detectives" and take turns asking the spy questions about the description and general location of the secret item. The questions must require no more than a "Yes" or "No" response. The group is given a limited time (3 to 5 minutes) to ask the questions. At the end of that time, the group must agree upon only one guess as to the identity of the object. If the group guesses wrong, the spy chooses another object for the group to guess. A correct guess allows another player to become the spy.

# *Twenty Questions*

**Objective:**

To guess a word by asking 20 or fewer yes-or-no questions about the word.

**Players:**

2 or more

**Ages:**

7 and up

**Materials:**

optional writing materials

**Setting:**

anywhere

**Directions:**

A player thinks of an object and tells the other players whether it is "animal," "vegetable," or "mineral," or a combination of any of these. "Animal" can include anything made from animals, such as a leather saddle. It can also include any living animal or person. "Vegetable" includes plants, plus anything made from plants, such as a wooden baseball bat. "Mineral" is anything metal or rock or made from minerals like a plastic snorkel or an aluminum can. The other players can ask up to a total of 19 questions about the object before naming it. The 20th question must be a guess. Any other guesses will be counted as one of the 20 questions. If the players cannot guess the object within the 20-question limit, the player who thought of the object gets to think of another object. When players guess the object within the 20-question limit, another player gets a turn to think of an object. Questions may be tallied on paper or on a chalkboard. An alternative scoring procedure is to tally only the "no" answers, up to 20, allowing players more opportunity to ask questions.

# 22

# *Name that Tune*

**Objective:**
To remember the titles of musical selections by listening to the first few bars.

**Players:**
4 or more

**Ages:**
8 and up

**Materials:**
records and record player or tapes and tape recorder

**Setting:**
indoors is easiest

**Directions:**
This game has several variations, which are described below. A leader is selected and takes charge of playing the tunes. If tapes and a tape recorder are used, tapes must be preset to play at the beginning of each selection. The leader plays the first few notes of a musical selection and stops the recorder. The other players are given a few seconds to recall and guess the name of the piece. If no one can think of a title, a few more bars are played and the music is stopped again, and so on until someone guesses the name of the tune.

Variations: Play each musical selection continuously until someone remembers and shouts out the title. If you have (and play) a piano, play a few notes or bars of a song and stop, or play continuously until someone guesses the tune. Ask someone who can "carry a tune" to sing the notes with "La-la-la's" instead of words.

# 23

# *Who, Me?*

**Objective:**

To keep the group's rhythm with clapping and slapping while remembering a number and a script.

**Players:**

8 or more

**Ages:**

8 and up

**Materials:**

**Setting:**

indoors or outdoors

**Directions:**

Players sit in a circle facing each other. One person is selected as the leader. The remaining players count off, remembering their own number. The leader begins the motions and sets the pace for the rhythm. The motions are: first slap the thighs with both hands, next clap hands, then snap the right finger-thumb, and finally snap the left finger-thumb. The leader may do this several times until the rest of the group catches the rhythm. Then the leader and players recite a script that follows the rhythm and motions. All words are spoken on the "slap thighs" and "clap hands" beats. The two finger snaps are "free" or "thinking time."

The leader begins by citing a number of one person in the group. For example, the leader may say (during the thigh slapping and hand clapping), "Number 4." The player who is number 4 must respond during the next thigh slap/hand clap, "Who, me?" The leader says back, in rhythm, "Yes, you." Number 4 responds again,

"Couldn't be." The leader returns with, "Then, who?" Number 4 ends by calling out another person's number, such as, "Number 8." The leader begins the chant all over again, this time speaking with Number 8. Players who get confused and miss the order of the script, are out. The last person left becomes the next leader. The game may also be played with no outs, so that everybody simply laughs at the confusion.

# 24

# *Cities*

**Objective:**
   To name a city in the world beginning with each letter of the alphabet.

**Players:**
   2 or more

**Ages:**
   9 and up

**Materials:**
   pencils and paper, atlases or other geographical reference books.

**Setting:**
   any place with writing surfaces

**Directions:**
   Have the players write the alphabet down the side of a piece of paper, using the back if necessary. When everyone is ready, signal the players to begin writing the names of world cities opposite the letters. The first player to finish shouts, "Finished!" and all the other players stop writing while that player reads his or her list aloud. If all names are valid city names, the first player to finish is declared a winner. If anyone challenges the accuracy of a city, ask the challenger to verify the listing in a reference book. Any mistake disqualifies the player and the remaining players continue the game until a second person finishes.

   The game may also be played with a time limit. At the end of an agreed-upon time period, the player with the most valid city names is declared the winner. Examples of city names for each letter of the alphabet include: A-Albany, B-Boston, C-Cleveland, D-Dallas,

E-Edinburgh, F-Frankfort, G-Gary, H-Houston, I-Indianapolis, J-Juneau, K-Karachi, L-Las Vegas, M-Memphis, N-New Delhi, O-Oakland, P-Paris, Q-Quebec, R-Rome, S-Salem, T-Tijuana, U-Utica, V-Venice, W-Waco, X-Xochimilco, Y-Youngstown, Z-Zurich. The game may be varied by restricting the geographical area under consideration to a single state, the United States, or countries outside of the United States.

# 25

# *Association*

**Objective:**
To guess a word or idea closely associated with one that is provided.

**Players:**
2 or more

**Age:**
7 and up

**Materials:**
3" x 5" cards, pencils

**Setting:**
indoors or outdoors

**Directions:**
Everyone is given an equal number of cards and a pencil. Players take several minutes to write word association pairs on the cards, one word on each side. For example, the association, "black and white," is written "black" on one side of the card and "white" on the other. Other examples of word association pairs are: "pork and beans", "ham and eggs", "cat and dog", "spic and span", "true and false", "bread and butter", "rock and roll", and "touch and go."

A player begins by holding up a card for the group to see. The first player to guess the word on the other side of the card gets to hold up one of his or her cards. Variation: Each player turns in two or three cards to a leader, who holds them up one at a time. The first player to shout out the correct associated word is given the card to hold.

# 26

# *Who Am I?*

**Objective:**
  To guess the name of a famous person by asking questions about that person.

**Players:**
  2 or more

**Age:**
  8 and up

**Materials:**
  none

**Setting:**
  anywhere

**Directions:**
  A player is chosen to represent a famous person. The person can be an historical figure, a movie star, a sports hero, a rock star, a mythical personality, or a character from a book. All the other players ask questions which the "famous person" can answer with "Yes" or "No." The questions may be about the famous person's gender, looks, life-style, occupation, personality, life events, and so on. The game can be limited to 15 or 20 questions or can proceed until someone correctly guesses the identity of the person. The player who makes the correct identification then gets an opportunity to represent a famous person.

# *COMMUNICATION GAMES*

Effective communication is arguably the most important element in the success of any group or any group endeavor. Communication games can help players learn important listening and speaking skills in the context of enjoyable experiments and simulations.

The ten games in this section focus on selected modes of communication—expressing (or coding) a message, transferring or passing on information, and receiving information. Verbal, auditory, visual, and tactile communication skills are exercised.

# 27

# *The Haunted House*

**Objective:**
To listen for cues in a story and act out the cue words.

**Number of players:**
minimum of 3 plus a storyteller, no maximum

**Ages:**
5 and up

**Materials:**
none

**Setting:**
room or outdoor area

**Directions:**
In this game, one person becomes the storyteller and makes up a story about a haunted house, using character- and object-words identified in advance by the group. For example, words could include *monster, coffin, clock, ghost, candle, cat, dracula, mummy, spider,* and *door*. The group decides on a sound and action with which to "act out" each of the identified words every time the storyteller mentions it in the story. For example, the word *clock* might be acted out with the sound "tick, tock" and the back-and-forth swaying of the body; the word *mummy* with straight posture, arms tightly against the sides, and a groaning sound; and the word *candle* with the forefingers wiggling and the words, "flicker, flicker." The storyteller begins the tale, making sure to include each identified word several times.

The game can be adapted to various size groups and different ages. In small groups, each player acts out a different word; in large groups, players are divided into teams, each team acting out a word. Additional variations include the use of more or fewer words, and multiple storytellers who take turns weaving a single tale.

# 28

# *Charades*

**Objective:**
To pantomime the name of a well known phrase, book, story, movie, famous person or T.V. show; to determine the meaning of non-verbal actions and gestures.

**Players:**
4 or more

**Ages:**
8 and up

**Materials:**
pencils and paper, paper bags or other containers

**Setting:**
room with chairs

**Directions:**
In this old English parlour game, the players divide into two teams. Each team meets in a separate corner of the room (or in a different room) to agree on a list of T.V. shows, movies, books, stories, or sentences to be acted out by the other team. The selections are written on separate slips of paper, which are then folded and placed in a container. Straws or numbers are drawn to determine which team goes first. A player from that team draws a slip of paper from the other team's container. The player is given 1 minute to read the paper and decide how to act out the title or sentence without giving verbal clues. The player can act out the whole idea, one word at a time, or one syllable at a time. A player from the opposing team keeps time and records how long it takes for the actor's team to guess the charade.

The time allotted for acting may be limited. Universal gestures may be determined in advance for both groups. For example, drawing a circle with both hands can represent a whole idea; holding up fingers can indicate the number of words in the name or sentence or the numerical order of the word being acted out; opening hands like a book can represent a book title; pointing to the head can stand for an idea or sentence, and putting a hand on one's chest can indicate a famous person. Limit younger players to story or book titles known by the whole group and determined by an adult leader.

# 29

# *Whispering Down the Lane*

**Objective:**

To observe and experience changes in a message as it is passed verbally from one person to another.

**Players:**

10 or more

**Ages:**

7 and up

**Materials:**

**Setting:**

any room or open outdoor area

**Directions:**

Players stand in a row or circle. The first player makes up a sentence which says who did what, with whom, where, and when. For example, the player might say, "Last week Mr. Rabbit sold peaches at the fair with old Mr. Toad." or "I saw Lisa play hopscotch with Jenny on the playground yesterday morning." The first player whispers the sentence to the next player in line who in turn tells it to the next player, and so on down the line (or around the circle). The last person to receive the message repeats it out loud to the group. The first player then restates the original sentence aloud, and the group identifies and discusses how the sentence has been changed. Players take turns making up new sentences, trying to make them as elaborate as possible to add to the confusion and fun.

# 30

# *Trust Walk*

**Objective:**

To silently guide a partner who is blindfolded; to explore an area with senses other than the sense of sight.

**Players:**

any number of pairs, an extra person forming one triad

**Ages:**

6 and up

**Materials:**

blindfolds for each pair

**Setting:**

outdoors

**Directions:**

Each player chooses a partner. One partner is blindfolded and the other serves as the guide. Without talking or establishing communication signals in advance, the guide leads the blindfolded partner around a designated area, providing opportunities for him or her to touch different objects, listen to sounds, and smell aromas and scents. The guide tries to establish nonverbal signals to indicate left, right, straight ahead, up, down, fast, slow, and so on. After 5 to 10 minutes, a timekeeper signals the partners to stop and change roles.

# 31

# *Musical Chairs*

**Objective:**
To engage players in an activity wherein they can pantomime and interact.

**Players:**
8 or more

**Ages:**
6 and up

**Materials:**
chairs and music (radio, record player and records, tape recorder and tapes, or a musical instrument)

**Setting:**
indoors or outdoors

**Directions:**
One person volunteers to play the music (radio, tape recorder, record player, or musical instrument). Players arrange their chairs in a circle facing out or in a row with every other chair facing backwards. There should be one less chair than players. When the music begins, the players walk or march around the chairs. The person playing the music stops the music without warning and everyone tries to sit in a chair. The player who does not get a chair is given the opportunity to "graduate" from the game by pantomiming an animal. The other players must guess the animal before they can resume the game. When they have guessed the animal, a chair is removed and the game resumes. The game continues in this way until one person is left. Older players may select occupations or another category to pantomime.

# 32

# *Passing the Object*

**Objective:**

To pass an imaginary object down a row of people by imitating the actions of the previous player and to guess the name of the object being passed.

**Players:**

5 or more

**Ages:**

7 and up

**Materials:**

**Setting:**

indoors or outdoors

**Directions:**

Players stand in line. The first player decides on an object, heavy or light, big or small, and pantomimes lifting it up and passing it on to the next player. Through the positioning and movement of her hands, the first player indicates the shape, size, and weight of the object being passed. The second player takes the imaginary object and tries to imitate the actions of the first person by lifting and passing the object to the third player in line. Each player, in turn, continues the movements until the last person receives the object. The last person then tries to guess what the object is. If he misses the guess, the next-to-last person guesses, and the guesses proceed backwards up the line. If the second person does not guess correctly, the first person reveals the object's identity. The first person then moves to the last position, each player moves up in line, and a new game begins.

# 33

# *Muk*

**Objective:**

To try to make another person laugh by making silly gestures and sounds or to try not to laugh when someone else is making silly gestures and sounds.

**Players:**

8 or more

**Ages:**

6 and up

**Materials:**

**Setting:**

indoors or outdoors

**Directions:**

This is an Eskimo game originally played in the Canadian Arctic. Its name, "Muk," means "silence" in Eskimo. A group of players sits in a circle. One person is chosen to be "It" and sits in the middle. When "It" points to someone in the circle, that person must say, "Muk." Then "It" tries to make her laugh by jumping around and making silly gestures, faces, and funny sounds. If that person laughs, she changes places with "It" and stands inside the circle. If she manages to keep silent, with a straight face, "It" must point to another person who says, "Muk," and tries to keep from laughing while "It" acts silly again.

For a group with more than 20 players, an adaptation of this game can be fun. Players form two equal lines facing each other, about 4 feet apart. One person is chosen to walk down the line while everyone else in line acts silly and tries to make him laugh. If he makes it all the way down the line without cracking a smile, he is granted the title "Muk King" (or "Muk Queen" for a girl). Each person takes a turn walking the "gauntlet" and trying to earn the title.

# 34

# *Simon Says*

**Objective:**

To imitate the motions of a leader upon hearing, "Simon says," and to hold a position if the leader makes a motion without saying, "Simon says."

**Players:**

3 or more

**Ages:**

6 and up

**Materials:**

**Setting:**

a spacious area indoors or outdoors

**Directions:**

A leader is chosen who stands in front of the other players and commands them to make certain movements with parts of their bodies, such as, "Put hands on your hips." The players obey her if she says, "Simon says" before giving the order. If she merely gives the order, players hold their last position. If a player moves or follows an order without hearing, "Simon says," he is "out." The leader tries to trick the other players by physically demonstrating a command that is not preceded by "Simon says," or by giving a "Simon says" order concerning one motion while physically demonstrating a different motion. For example, she might say, "Simon says, lift your knee" and, at the same time, lift her elbow. The last player "out" is the leader for the next game.

# 35

# *Strength Bombardment*

**Objective:**

To acknowledge other persons for their strengths.

**Players:**

5 or more

**Ages:**

7 and up

**Materials:**

**Setting:**

indoors or outdoors

**Directions:**

Players sit or stand in a circle. One person is chosen to be the "target." Each of the other players must think of something that the "target" has said or done that demonstrates a positive trait or strength of character. For example, one person might state that the "target" smiled at her earlier in the day. Another person might remember a game in which the "target" went to the end of the line without arguing, even though he had been called "out" by mistake. Still another player might recall hearing the "target" say kind words to an injured and crying child. After being allowed a few moments to think, players take turns telling the "target" about the positive things he has done to show strength of character. When everyone has "bombarded" the "target" with acknowledgements, another person is selected to be "target." The game continues until everyone has experienced a "strength bombardment."

# 36

# *Listening Game*

**Objective:**
To role play "non-listening" and "active listening" behaviors.

**Players:**
2 or more

**Ages:**
9 and up

**Materials:**
none

**Setting:**
indoors or outdoors

**Directions:**
Players find partners. An extra person may be asked to join a pair, forming one triad. Players decide on two topics to talk about, one for each partner. Examples of simple topics include, "My Favorite Animal," "A Movie I Saw," "What I Did Over the Weekend," and "What I Would Do If I Were President." Partners decide who is the first "talker." The other partner plays the "listener." The game has two rounds, each consisting of two 3-minute parts.

Round 1, Part 1: The talker begins to discuss one of the topics. The listener does everything *but* listen. He interrupts, fidgets with his hands and legs, doesn't face or look at the talker, focuses his attention on other discussions, and generally displays non-listening behaviors. The talker tries to concentrate on the topic without laughing or showing anger at the unattending listener. Round 1, Part 2: After three minutes, the talker discusses the topic again, and the listener demonstrates "active listening" behaviors—facing the talker, maintaining good eye contact, nodding and responding at appropriate times, repeating phrases to clarify ideas, keeping hands and feet still, and leaning slightly toward the talker. Round 2: The partners switch roles so that the talker becomes the listener and vice versa. Both parts of the second round follow the same procedure as the first round, except that the talker discusses the second topic. At the conclusion of both rounds, the partners may be directed to join other players for a group discussion contrasting non-listening with active listening behaviors.

# *COOPERATIVE GAMES*

Although cooperation and collaboration are emphasized throughout this entire book, some games are specifically designed to develop the skills required for truly collaborative efforts. Use these games as team-building exercises and maximize their impact with follow-up discussions.

The games in this section are useful in contrasting cooperative behaviors with competitive behaviors and for encouraging players to focus on group rather than individual tasks.

# 37

# *Skin the Snake*

**Objective:**
To connect and move with a whole group in order to accomplish a physical task.

**Players:**
8 to 10 minimum

**Ages:**
8 and up

**Materials:**
none

**Setting:**
a large grassy area, or a large room with tumbling mats end-to-end

**Directions:**
Players line up one behind another, the more the merrier. All players in line reach between their legs with their left hand and grab the right hand of the person behind them, creating a human chain. Once the players are connected, the last person in line slowly lies down on his back. The other players begin to waddle backwards. When the next-to-last person straddles the body of the player on the ground and becomes the last in line, she lies down, with hands still clasped to the persons in front and behind her. The snake is skinned when everyone is lying down with hands connected. The snake can recover itself by reversing the movements. The last to lie down gets up and starts waddling forward, pulling the rest of the group up and forward until the original chain is reformed. The game can be played as a relay between two large teams. The only rule is that if anyone breaks hands during any part of the process, that person must stop and reconnect before moving again.

# 38

# *Broken Hearts*

**Objective:**
To assemble identical hearts from parts distributed randomly to a group.

**Players:**
unlimited groups with 4 to 8 members each

**Age:**
8 and up

**Materials:**
red construction paper, scissors, pencils, heart pattern (optional)

**Setting:**
indoors, with a table for each group of 4 to 8

**Directions:**
One person in each group creates a heart pattern for the others to trace by folding a piece of construction paper in half and cutting a half-heart shape. All other players in the group trace the heart on a piece of red construction paper and cut it out, creating identical hearts. Working individually, each player then cuts his or her heart into 4 pieces. All of the pieces are then pooled, scrambled, and redistributed equally among the players. Each person must now assemble a heart using the redistributed pieces. The game is played in complete silence. Players may *give away* pieces to other members of the group, but NO ONE can *take* or *ask for* a piece from another player, either verbally or through the use of nonverbal gestures. The game is over when every player has assembled a heart. Groups may wish to time each successive game to note improvements in performance.

# 39

# *Stand Up Together*

**Objective:**

To stand up, back-to-back with a partner or teammates, from a sitting position on the ground.

**Players:**

Minimum of 2

**Ages:**

6 and up

**Materials:**

**Setting:**

an open grassy area or room with tumbling mats

**Directions:**

Players divide into pairs. Partners sit on the ground, back-to-back, knees bent and elbows linked. From that position, both partners lean together against each other's back and slowly push with the legs to get to a standing position. Struggling, stumbling, and giggling is expected until partners get the feel of how to balance themselves and move as a unit. Once the move is mastered in pairs, add a third person to each group, then another, and another. The game can also be played with a large group standing shoulder-to shoulder tightly in a circle. However, unless the whole group is seriously concentrating on the task, be ready to witness more giggling and stumbling than standing!

# 40

# *People Pyramids*

**Objective:**
  To build and sustain a pyramid using the bodies of players.

**Players:**
  6 or more

**Ages:**
  8 and up

**Materials:**
  optional camera

**Setting:**
  a grassy area outdoors or a large room with tumbling mats

**Directions:**
  Form teams of six and proceed as follows: The three huskiest
  players line up shoulder-to-shoulder on their hands and knees,
  keeping their backs straight. The two next-huskiest players
  carefully climb onto the backs of the first three. Each of these
  players straddles two of the lower players, placing hands on the
  shoulders and knees and feet on the backs (next to, but not on the
  spine) of the lower players. The lightest person tops off the pyramid
  by climbing on and straddling the two middle players. Players try
  to "hold" the position for at least 15 seconds, allowing enough time
  to snap a picture of the pyramid if a camera is available. To break
  up the pyramid, players collapse and roll toward the outside of the
  configuration. A group of 10 can make a larger pyramid, with four
  on the bottom, then three, two, and one. Ambitious groups can
  make a castle by creating a circular base with players facing inward
  and two to three layers on top.

# 41

# *The Lap Game*

**Objective:**

To form a line or circle of people in which all persons simultaneously sit on the lap of the person behind them.

**Players:**

8 minimum, no maximum

**Ages:**

8 and up

**Materials:**

**Setting:**

a grassy area outdoors

**Directions:**

Players line up facing the same direction, hands on the waist of the person in front of them. The last player in line releases her hands from the person in front of her and lies down on her back with her feet on the ground and her knees bent. The next to the last person carefully backs up and sits on the last player's raised knees. The next person up the line then moves backwards and sits on the lap of the next to last person, and so on until everyone is sitting on the lap of the person behind. The larger the group, the more challenging it is to have everyone sitting at the same time. Players can also line up in a tight circle and all try to sit at the same time without anyone falling or bungling.

# 42

# *Group Story*

**Objective:**
To include every member of a group in telling or writing a story.

**Players:**
2 or more

**Ages:**
8 and up

**Materials:**
paper and pencils if writing a story

**Setting:**
indoors or outdoors

**Directions:**
Players begin by deciding on a theme for their story. Then, one player begins the story by describing the setting in as much detail as possible. A second player introduces and describes the characters. A third player creates the problem to be solved or the goal to be attained in the story. A fourth player begins a series of obstacle/ solution events. Elaboration of the story continues, encompassing the contributions of as many people as are in the group. The last person concludes the story by bringing all of the pieces together. If the story is written, the paper is passed from one person to the next. The last person finishes the story and hands the paper to the first person, who reads the story to the group. It is fun to hear how a story changes from one person to the next, and how it finally ends. An adaptation of this idea involves creating a group painting or drawing in which each player adds a new element to the picture. Either the storytelling/writing game or its graphic adaptation can be played by as few as two people, with players taking turns until both agree that the story or picture is finished.

# 43

# *Stack Up*

**Objective:**
To move one chair to the right if your answer to a given question is, "Yes," and to move one chair to the left if your answer is, "No." To attempt, by asking questions, to get everyone sitting on each other's lap in a single chair.

**Players:**
6 or more

**Ages:**
7 and up

**Materials:**
as many chairs as players, except for the leader

**Setting:**
a large room or outdoor area

**Directions:**
One player is selected to be the "Caller." All remaining players sit in chairs in a circle. The Caller's job is to ask a series of questions of the group. If a player's answer is, "No," he remains in his chair. If a player's answer is, "Yes," she moves one seat to the right, regardless of whether or not someone is sitting in the chair. If someone is in the chair, she simply sits on that person's lap. The Caller asks questions such as, "Do you like broccoli?," "Were you born in this state?," "Do you have a dog?," "Are there younger brothers or sisters in your family?" The Caller tries to second guess the answers of the players so that they all end up in one chair on each other's lap. For example, the Caller might ask questions with obvious answers like, "Do you like free time?," "Would you rather have a new Ferrari than an old Plymouth?," "Do you like chocolate better than licorice?" When the Caller succeeds in manipulating the questions so that everyone is stacked up, a new game begins.

# 44

# *Caterpillar*

**Objective:**

To create a caterpillar-like movement with a large group of people rolling over each other on the ground.

**Players:**

many, but a minimum of 10

**Ages:**

6 and up

**Materials:**

**Setting:**

a grassy area outdoors or a large room with tumbling mats

**Directions:**

All players lie down side-by-side on their stomachs, as close together as possible, and with their arms outstretched over their heads. A player at one end of the row begins to roll over all the other players. He continues rolling until he reaches the end of the bodies, where he once again lies on his stomach, becoming the end person. Then the next person begins rolling across the bodies. When she is about halfway across the row of bodies, a third person may begin to roll. As the rolling proceeds, players initiate their rolls as soon as they are first in line, creating a caterpillar-like movement across the ground. When players run out of space, reverse the movement of the caterpillar.

# 45

# *Walking*

**Objective:**
To take a walk and observe things in a different way.

**Players:**
2 or more

**Ages:**
5 and up

**Materials:**
none

**Setting:**
outdoors

**Directions:**
Go for a walk with one or more family members or friends.
Observe things in a different way by playing one of the following
mini-games: Look for beautiful objects. See who can name the
most beautiful things like plants, houses, windows, cars, and
landscape designs. Or play a "What's wrong?" game. Look for
things that can be fixed, changed, or corrected to make them "right,"
like weeds, cracks in driveways, broken windows, dirty cars, and
dried-up plants. Another way to take a walk is to have every other
person walk backwards, and to share the differences in what is
observed. Or take a bird-watching walk. See who can spot the
most birds or varieties of birds. Walk in a new neighborhood and
make up stories about, "Who Lives in This House?" Count dogs or
cats while walking. Finally, try to walk in a new way by changing
to a step-together-step, skip, hop left (3 times) and hop right (3
times).

# 46

# *Lean-To*

**Objective:**
To form a stable "lean-to" circle by holding hands and leaning in opposite directions.

**Players:**
8 or more

**Ages:**
8 and up

**Materials:**
none

**Setting:**
a grassy open area

**Directions:**
All players join hands in a circle, the more the better. Players count off by two's ("one, two, one, two," etc.). An odd person may step inside the circle and become the "Caller." Otherwise, any player can become the Caller. When the Caller says, "Lean-to," the 1's slowly lean inward and the 2's lean outward. With hands held tightly, they should form an equally balanced "lean-to." This move may take a little practice to perfect. When it is accomplished to everyone's satisfaction, the Caller says, "Lean-to" again and the players switch leaning positions, the 2's leaning inward and the 1's leaning outward. When the players find switching back and forth easy, they can add the extra challenge of a "Left" or "Right" rotating movement.

# *Centipede*

**Objective:**
To move a group of players like a centipede, walking on hands, with legs wrapped around one another's waists.

**Players:**
4 or more

**Ages:**
7 and up

**Materials:**
none

**Setting:**
A grassy outdoor area

**Directions:**
Players sit down on the grass, one behind the other. Each player wraps her legs around the waist of the player in front of her to form the body of the centipede. Each player's arms become a set of legs for the centipede. When someone gives a signal, all players lift themselves off the ground with their hands and scoot along, like a giant centipede. Anyone who disconnects must shout, "Stop! Reconnect" and everyone waits for that person to reconnect. Large groups may divide into teams, making two or more centipedes, and race between a start and finish line. Centipedes may also decide on a "team noise" to make while scuttling across the field.

# Spiral

**Objective:**
To form a winding and unwinding human spiral using a line of people.

**Players:**
15 or more

**Ages:**
5 and up

**Materials:**
none

**Setting:**
outdoors

**Directions:**
Players form a circle and join hands. Two adjoining players break hands to create a head and tail. The tail stands still while the head leads the rest of the line in a spiraling motion around the tail. The line of players coils around the tail until all players are wrapped snugly around one another and the head cannot move any further. The tail leads in unwinding the spiral from the inside out, ducking or crawling under the arms and legs of other players without breaking hands. Everyone follows the tail to remake the big circle. Anyone who breaks hands must yell, "Stop," until hands are rejoined; then, "Okay," to resume. The game may be played again with a different head and tail, and with the head leading the spiral in a different direction.

# *GET-ACQUAINTED GAMES*

The games in this section were selected because they encourage self-disclosure and sharing in the non-threatening context of play. They can be used to help students become better acquainted, to promote inclusion, to build team cohesiveness, or as preludes to more challenging tasks. Players introduce themselves to one or more persons, focusing on the value of each individual and acknowledging similarities and differences.

# 49

# *My Name is Molly...*

**Objective:**

To learn each others' names by using mnemonic devices and to test memory capacity. This game is an adaptation of the old memory games such as "Grandmother's Trunk" and "I Packed My Bag."

**Players:**

minimum of 3 (Maximum depends on age level and time constraints; however, 10 to 20 can be fun for children 8 and up.)

**Ages:**

6 and up

**Materials:**

**Setting:**

a room with chairs arranged in a circle, square, or other simple configuration.

**Directions:**

In this game, players get to know each other by associating their first names with animal names that begin with the same letter. Arrange chairs in a circle or other simple configuration, and designate one player to be the first to introduce himself. That player begins by saying, "Hello. My name is (first name), and I like (name of an animal that begins with the same letter). The second player must reintroduce the first player, repeating his name and animal, e.g., "His name is... (Harry) and he likes... (hyenas)." Then the second player gives her name and the animal she likes that begins with the same letter. Each time a new player introduces him/herself, that player must first repeat, in order, the names and animals of all of the previous players. Go around the group until each person has had a turn, ending with the first person. If time permits, go around a second time so that everyone can have an opportunity to repeat the names and animals of *all* players. Players may assist any person who forgets a name by giving a hint such as the first letter of the player's name or the second letter of the animal's name. Players whose names start with the same letter must choose different animals.

Older participants may enjoy this more challenging adaptation: Players give their name followed by a verb *and* animal name, all beginning with the same letter, thus making funny, nonsensical sentences like "My name is Terri and I tickle tigers."

# 50

# *People Treasure Hunt*

**Objective:**

To assist children in getting to know something about each other and in communicating with each other.

**Players:**

The more the merrier. This game is ideal for a classroom of 20 to 36 children.

**Ages:**

8 and up

**Setting:**

classroom or other large room

**Materials:**

one copy per player of the "People Treasure Hunt" (modified to suit the interests and age levels of players); pencils.

**Directions:**

Each player receives a copy of the "People Treasure Hunt" and a pencil. When the leader signals the game to begin, players walk around the room asking each other if they fit any of the criteria on the list. When someone matches a criterion, she writes her name on the line next to the trait. The only rule is that a player may sign another player's list just one time—for one trait. This is likely to necessitate some erasing and switching names in the course of the game, as players attempt to match each trait to a different person. A player may sign his own list if he is the youngest, oldest, etc.

As players finish and their lists are checked by the leader, they can become "checkers" or be sent out to help another player complete his or her list.

# People Treasure Hunt

**Find a person who:**

1. Is older than you.

2. Wears Nike running shoes.

3. Has never eaten brussels sprouts.

4. Has more brothers than you.

5. Is shorter than you.

6. Knows how to swim.

7. Wears pierced earrings.

8. Has fewer letters in his/her last name than you have in yours.

9. Likes pepperoni pizza.

10. Knows all of the words of the "Star Spangled Banner."

11. Is younger than you.

12. Has a bottom that is higher off the floor than yours.

13. Owns a dog.

14. Has never been to an amusement (theme) park.

15. Can curl his/her tongue.

# 51

# *And Now Presenting...*

**Objective:**

To allow partners to get to know each other and to introduce each other to a larger group.

**Players:**

5 to 15 pairs (an extra can form a triad, if necessary)

**Ages:**

8 and up

**Materials:**

pencils and paper

**Setting:**

a room with chairs and desks, tables, or lapboards

**Directions:**

Each player chooses a partner that she does not know. She then has 5 minutes to "interview" her partner, asking questions about the partner's interests, hobbies, strengths, wishes, goals, and family/home life. The interviewer can take notes on paper to capture important details. A timekeeper gives the signal to start and stop. The interviewers then have 1 minute to stand up before the group and introduce their partner, presenting any pertinent or interesting information as part of the introduction. The partners then switch roles, and the other half of the players is interviewed and introduced.

If the group is larger than 20, or if the players have difficulty sitting for a long time, complete the first and second halves of the interviews at different times of the day or on two separate days.

For younger children, the leader may develop and duplicate a simple interview sheet for the interviewers to complete. Some possible interview questions are: *What is your full name? Do you have a nickname? What is your favorite color (subject, sport, T.V. program, singer, car, animal)? How many brothers and sisters do you have? What are you good at? If you could get better in any area, what would it be? How old are you? If you could be anyone else, who would you be?*

# 52

# *I Like My New Friend*

**Objective:**

To learn the name of a new acquaintance and to validate that person with a positive descriptive word.

**Players:**

from a group of 5 or 6 to a larger group of 25 or more

**Ages:**

9 and up

**Materials:**

some dictionaries

**Setting:**

classroom, large room, or outdoor area

**Directions:**

Players sit in a large circle. They are directed to turn to the person on their right and ask that person's name. Any player begins the game by saying, "I like my new friend (name of the person on their right), with a (first letter of that person's name) because s/he is so (a positive descriptive word beginning with that same letter)." For example, the player might say, "I like my new friend Janelle with a J because she is so jolly." The process is continued around the circle until the first player is named and given a positive word. Players may need time to look up adjectives in the dictionary if they cannot think of a positive word to say to their new friend.

# 53

# *Personal Totem Poles*

**Objective:**
To introduce oneself to others by creating and sharing a six-layered totem pole symbolizing personal traits and choices.

**Players:**
2 and up

**Ages:**
6 to 13

**Materials:**
12" x 18" white construction paper, 1 sheet per person; scissors, stapler; colored pencils, markers, or crayons

**Setting:**
room with tables or desks and chairs

**Directions:**
Each participant creates a personal totem pole from a piece of white construction paper folded in half lengthwise and cut along the fold. The participant folds each strip in thirds to create a total of six sections and staples the two strips end-to-end. Turning the strip to a vertical position and using colored pencils, markers, or crayons, each person designs a personal totem pole. Each section is filled in with a picture or symbol representing a personality trait, like or dislike, strength, weakness, wish, or ambition. Leaders working with younger children may present a list of 6 items for the children to symbolize or draw; for example: 1) Favorite food (book, song, singer, game, T.V. program), 2) What I want to be when I grow up, 3) A Wish, 4) If I Were an Animal I'd be..., 5) I'm afraid of..., 6) What I do best. When the personal totem poles are finished, participants share them with the whole group or in smaller groups as a way of introducing themselves.

# 54

# *Categories*

**Objective:**

To allow players to become better acquainted with each other and to give each player a sense of inclusion

**Players:**

small to large group, the more the merrier

**Ages:**

5 and up

**Materials:**

**Setting:**

room with chairs or grassy outdoor area

**Directions:**

Players sit in a circle. A leader is chosen who calls out categories into which one or more players fit. When a category is named, players who fit that category stand in place. Suggested categories include: Persons who: ...know how to turn a somersault, ...are wearing white socks, ...have brown eyes, ...like to swim, ...have a baby brother or sister, ...have ridden an airplane, ...like spinach, ...have a cat at home, ...were born in another country. After several categories are named and players have stood up and down many times, a more active version of the game may be played. In the new game, when the leader calls out a category, players stand up and exchange seats with others in the same category. The leader also tries to find a seat vacated by a player, which leaves one person without a seat. That person becomes the new leader, stands in the middle, and calls out a new category.

Older children may enjoy another form of this game in which the categories are written on sheets of butcher paper and posted around the room. The players walk around the room and sign their names to categories that fit them.

# 55

# *Personal Time Line*

**Objective:**
To create a timeline, highlighting special events in one's life; to share the timeline as a way of introducing oneself to a group.

**Players:**
2 or more

**Ages:**
8 and up

**Materials:**
2 or more sheets of 8 1/2" x 11" paper; stapler, scotch tape, or glue; rulers; pencils

**Setting:**
a room with tables or outdoor area with tables

**Directions:**
Each player takes one or more pieces of paper and lays it horizontally on a table. Pieces may be attached to each other with staples, glue, or scotch tape. Using a ruler, each player draws a "life line" across the paper, leaving a small space below the line to write in ages or dates and a large space above the line to write in important events. Equidistant vertical lines are drawn for each year of the player's life. The year or age of the player is labeled below each of the vertical lines.

Each player creates his or her personal time line by writing one or more significant events above the life line. Writing is most easily accomplished by turning the paper sideways and writing a description of each event to the right of the year or age in which the event occurred.  Events could include learning to walk, being potty trained, seeing an elephant for the first time, taking a special trip, moving to another place, meeting a new friend, starting school, learning to ride a two-wheeler, winning an award, and so on.  After the time lines are completed, each player shares his or her timeline with the rest of the group.

# 56

## *Seven-Up*

**Objective:**
To guess the identity of the person who tapped your thumb when your eyes were covered.

**Players:**
14 or more

**Ages:**
5 and up

**Materials:**
none

**Setting:**
indoors with tables or desks

**Directions:**
Players may wear name tags if they are not familiar with one another's names. Seven players are selected to be the first "tappers." They line up at one end of the playing area. One is selected as the leader. When the leader calls out, "Heads down, thumbs up," all of the players seated at tables and desks put their heads down on their arms, and raise the thumb of one clenched fist. Next, the seven "tappers" tiptoe around the room quietly, each tapping one person's thumb. When all seven are finished, they line up again, and the leader calls out, "Seven-up." The seven who were tapped stand up. One by one, the leader calls on them and each guesses who tapped his or her thumb. If a player guesses correctly, he changes places with the tapper. If the guess is incorrect, the player takes a seat. When all seven have guessed, the game begins again. When someone guesses the leader correctly, she becomes the new leader.

# *IMAGINATION GAMES*

The games in this section were selected because of their ability to tap the imagination. Players must create scenarios, stories, and role plays with few props and little assistance. The focus is on divergent and creative thinking—and anyone capable of experiencing fantasy is an instant winner.

# 57

# *Name Exchange*

**Objective:**

To switch similar first names of famous people in order to form a different "image" of each.

**Players:**

2 or more

**Ages:**

10 and up

**Materials:**

optional history or reference books

**Setting:**

anywhere

**Directions:**

A player thinks of a famous person with a "formal" first name, such as "Elizabeth" Taylor, and then must think of another famous person whose first name is a "nickname" of the first person's name; for example, "Betsy" Ross. The player then calls out the names of the two famous people, switching first names. For example, the new names, "Betsy Taylor" and "Elizabeth Ross," create new "images" of both personalities. All other players take a turn creating similar newly named personalities. Examples of other name exchanges might be *Michael Mouse* and *Mickey Jordan, Billy the Conqueror* and *William the Kid, Jonathan Appleseed* and *Johnny Winters, King Davey* and *David Crockett, Charles Brown* and *Prince Charlie*, and so on. To stretch imaginations further, have the person who made the name switch describe the new images of the famous people.

# 58

# *New Year's Resolutions*

**Objective:**
   To create a New Year's Resolution for a famous person or character.

**Players:**
   2 or more

**Ages:**
   8 and up

**Materials:**
   optional writing materials

**Setting:**
   anywhere

**Directions:**
   Players choose a category of people for which they would like to create New Year's Resolutions. Possible categories include movie stars, rock or other music stars, historic personalities, or characters from books, cartoons, comic strips, T.V. shows, or nursery rhymes. Each player chooses a character from the selected category and says (or writes) a New Year's Resolution for that person. After the resolutions have been shared, another category may be chosen for a new game. As an alternative, the entire group may brainstorm resolutions for each character, creating a collaborative product instead of individual ones.

# 59

# *Hot Seat*

**Objective:**
To take the role of a character in a story and answer questions from the point of view of that character.

**Players:**
3 or more

**Ages:**
8 and up

**Materials:**
none

**Setting:**
indoors or outdoors

**Directions:**
Together, the group chooses a story that everyone knows, such as a fairy tale. One player is selected to play the role of a main character in the story. If the group is large, every character in the story can be represented by a player. The chosen players take a seat in front of the rest of the group. This is known as the "Hot Seat." While in the Hot Seat, a person must try to think and talk like the character he or she represents.

The game begins with the audience asking questions concerning events in the story. For example, if the "Hot Seat" were occupied by Little Red Riding Hood, her grandmother, the wolf, and the huntsman, the audience might ask questions about each character's behaviors, motives, and feelings in the story. The "play characters" answer the questions as if they really are the story characters, defending their actions and criticizing or praising the behaviors of their fellow "play characters." The game ends after all questions have been answered or a time limit has been reached. The next game features a different story and new "play characters" on the "Hot Seat." Other story suggestions include *Cinderella*, *The Three Little Pigs*, *Snow White*, *Jack and the Beanstalk*, or any other story or book the players have all read or heard.

# 60

# *Broomstick*

**Objective:**
To pantomime creative uses for a broomstick.

**Players:**
2 or more

**Ages:**
7 and up

**Materials:**
a broom handle, yardstick, pointer, or other long stick

**Setting:**
indoors or outdoors

**Directions:**
The first player takes a long stick, such as a broom handle or yardstick, and pantomimes an action using the stick. For example, he might act out using the stick as a fishing pole. The other players guess how the stick is being used, before passing the stick to the next player. The second player acts out another use of the stick, such as throwing a javelin or spear and, again, the group guesses. Each successive player in turn acts out a new use for the stick. The game continues until the group runs out of ideas or a time limit is reached. Other uses for the stick include a witch's broom, yardstick, mop, rifle, fence or sign post, fly swatter, conductor's wand, fairy wand, baton, and so on. To vary the game, follow the same steps using a hoop or frisbee instead of a stick.

# 61

# *How Do You Walk?*

**Objective:**

To walk with creative movements in response to cues called out by players in the group.

**Players:**

5 or more

**Ages:**

6 and up

**Materials:**

**Setting:**

outdoors

**Directions:**

Players line up side-by-side and begin walking. The person on the far left begins the game by calling out, "How do you walk if you are...?" and then adds a word or phrase to complete the question such as, "on hot sand." Then everyone creates his or her own movement to fit the sentence. Movements do not have to be identical, just appropriate to the meaning of the sentence. After a few seconds, the person to the right of the starting player calls out, "How do you walk if you are...?" and finishes the sentence. Each time the actions are changed, the next person to the right becomes the caller. Sentence enders may include: "on a tree limb," "on eggshells," "a tightrope walker," "a robot," "in quicksand," "on broken glass," "on glue," "on someone's back," "in deep snow," "with a broken leg," "when your house is on fire," "alone in a deserted alley," and "with rubber legs." When players run out of space, they turn around and head back the other way.

# 62

# *Moods*

**Objective:**
To express oneself with creative movements to different kinds of music.

**Players:**
1 or more

**Ages:**
all ages

**Materials:**
a variety of music on tapes, records, or CD's; sound system

**Setting:**
spacious room or outdoor area

**Directions:**
Player or players select various pieces of music that represent different moods and play them on an appropriate sound system. Some suggestions are:

- Happy: Tchaikovsky's "Nutcracker Suite"
- Sad: Many country music songs
- Angry: Greig's "March of the Mountain King"
- Playful: Saint-Saens' "Carnival Overture"
- Scary: Mussorgsky's "Night on Bald Mountain"
- Confident: Theme from "Star Wars"

Players listen to and interpret the mood of the music by moving their bodies in various ways. Players are encouraged to explore all levels of space by lying down, sitting, dancing around, jumping, leaping, and so on. To add more movement and color to the experience, scarves may be held and waved by the players. Partners may share their creative dances by holding hands, touching, and looking at each other with facial expressions that fit the music.

# 63

# *Lemonade*

**Objective:**
  To act out an occupation particular to a place; to avoid being tagged when someone guesses the trade and chases you.

**Players:**
  6 or more

**Ages:**
  6 and up

**Materials:**
  none

**Setting:**
  an open area outdoors

**Directions:**
  Players divide into two teams and line up facing each other about 15 yards apart. (Whether drawn, designated with markers, or merely remembered, each team is now standing on its own goal line.) One team starts out as the "Actors" and the other as the "Guessers." The Actors huddle together and decide on a city, state, or country and a trade or occupation indigenous to that place. For example, they might choose to represent jazz musicians from New Orleans, lobster fishermen from Maine, or rice farmers from China.

  To begin the game, the Actors take a giant step toward the Guessers and yell loudly, "Here we come!" Next, the Guessers take a giant step toward the Actors, yelling, "Where from?" Stepping again, the Actors answer the name of the place they chose. The Guessers

take another step and ask, "What's your trade?" The Actors take
the last step and call out together, "Lemonade!" Then they act
out their interpretation of the trade or occupation they chose. The
Guessers stay in their places and call out guesses as to what they
think the Actors are doing. As soon as a Guesser shouts out the
right occupation, the Actors panic and run back to their goal line.
The Guessers run after them and try to tag them. Whoever is tagged
before reaching his or her goal line becomes a member of the
opposite team. The game continues at the goal lines as the Actors
become the Guessers and vice versa.

# 64

# *Follow the Leader*

**Objective:**
To mimic the actions of a given leader and to take turns being the leader.

**Players:**
2 or more

**Ages:**
5 to 9

**Materials:**
none

**Setting:**
outdoors

**Directions:**
Players line up behind each other; the first in line is the leader. All players must follow the leader wherever he goes and imitate his actions. He may run, hop, skip, waddle, spin, move his arms and legs in fun ways, and/or imitate the motions of animals, machines, or people in their daily jobs. Anyone who does not mimic the actions of the leader must go to the end of the line. The second player in line gets a turn after a set period of time. The game can be varied by having all players hold hands while following the leader. Anyone who releases a hand during the game must go to the end of the line.

# NUMBER GAMES

All games have a mathematical basis. When the number of possible moves, players, and other factors are known, any strategy can be calculated in advance and expressed numerically. Even the winning strategy for a game like Tic-Tac-Toe can be stated in mathematical terms. Encouraging students to play with numbers helps mitigate some of the dread they feel when faced with math problems and concepts.

The games in this section have been chosen to stimulate an awareness of number patterns, develop spatial relationships, engage players in number operations, and to create an attitude of "number fun."

# 65

# *Buzz*

**Objective:**

To say, "Buzz," whenever a certain multiple is reached when counting around in a circle.

**Players:**

2 or more

**Ages:**

7 and up

**Materials:**

**Setting:**

indoors or outdoors

**Directions:**

Players sit in a circle and decide on a number greater than 2 to be the "Buzz" number. The number 5 is an easy number for younger children. Seven is popular among older kids. A first player is chosen and begins counting off. Each person in turn calls out the next number in sequence. If a player's number is a multiple of 7 or has the number 7 in it, that player must say, "Buzz," instead of naming the number. Any player who says 7 or a multiple of 7 instead of "Buzz" is out of the game.

Older children may enjoy the additional challenge created by choosing a second number to add to the game. One number is the "Buzz" number and the other is the "Fizz" number. For example, if the group chooses 5 and 7, any player whose number is a multiple of 5 or has 5 in it must say, "Buzz," and anyone whose number is a multiple of 7 or contains a 7 must say, "Fizz." When a number is a multiple of both, such as 35, or is made up of both numbers, such as 57, the player must say, "Buzz-Fizz." A third number may be added with its own sound, like "Splat," creating an even more hilarious, confusing game.

# 66

# *Slap, Clap, Snap*

**Objective:**
To say one's own number, then another player's number, while keeping the rhythm of the group's slapping, clapping, and snapping.

**Players:**
5 or more

**Ages:**
8 and up

**Materials:**
none

**Setting:**
outdoors in a grassy area or indoors

**Description:**
Players sit in a circle and "count off." Each player must remember his or her own number. A leader begins the motions and sets the rhythm, which consists of slapping both hands on the upper legs one time, clapping the hands once, snapping the right fingers once, then snapping the left fingers. The count is done to a 4/4 rhythm, slow at first and speeded up as the players join in and become comfortable with the motions.

The leader begins the play by saying his number, "one," at the same time he snaps his right finger. He then calls out another player's number while snapping the left finger. The player who has that number must be ready to repeat her number at the next snap of the right finger and another person's number at the snap of the left finger. Any player who calls numbers in the wrong order or confuses the motions when it is his or her turn, is out until the next round.

# 67

# *Merry-Go-Round*

**Objective:**
To apply any number from 1 to 39 to a mathematical formula, and to determine how many steps it takes to return to the original number.

**Players:**
1 or more

**Ages:**
8 and up

**Materials:**
pencils and paper

**Setting:**
anywhere there is a writing surface.

**Directions:**
Each player chooses one number between 1 and 39 and applies it to the following formula until the original number is reached again: Take the digit in the one's place (the farthest to the right) and multiply it by 4. Then add the digit (if any) in the ten's place to that product. Keep repeating the process to find out how many steps it takes to arrive at the original number. For example, take the number **23**. Multiply the digit in the one's place (**3**) by four (**3x4=12**). Now add that product (**12**) to the digit in the ten's place (**12+2=14**). Take that new number (**14**) and apply it to the formula (**4x4=16; 16+1=17**). Continue in the same way until the original number, **23**, is reached again (**7x4=28; 28+1=29**); (**9x4+36; 36+2=38**); (**8x4=32; 32+3=35**); (**5x4=20; 20+3=23**). The "Merry-Go-Round" has returned to **23**. Players may choose different numbers and compare how many steps it takes to return to the original number.

# Nim

**Objective:**
To force the other player into picking up the last object.

**Players:**
two

**Ages:**
8 and up

**Materials:**
minimum of 9 toothpicks, popsicle sticks, coins, pebbles, or similar objects

**Setting:**
any flat surface

**Directions:**
This is an ancient Chinese game given its name in 1901 by a mathematics professor at Harvard University. Players arrange sticks or other similar objects in rows containing different numbers. Nine sticks might be arranged to form a row of two, a row of three, and a row of four. Another design might be a row each of one, two, three, four, and five. Still another might consist of rows of three, five, and seven.

The first player begins by picking up any number of objects in any single row, including the entire row. The other player follows suit. The game continues until one player forces the other to pick up the last object. A variation of the game involves placing 15, 21, or 25 objects in a single row. Each player is allowed to pick up one, two, or three adjacent objects at a time until one player forces the other to pick up the last object.

# 69

# *Indian Cards*

**Objective:**
To guess, by reading other people's faces, if your card is high or low and place a bet on that guess.

**Players:**
4 or more

**Ages:**
9 and up

**Materials:**
a deck of cards and counters such as pebbles, poker chips, or pennies

**Setting:**
indoors around a table or on the floor

**Directions:**
Everyone sits around a table or in a circle on the floor. Players rotate being the dealer. The first dealer shuffles the cards and deals everyone a single card face down and calls out, "High," or "Low," indicating whether the high or the low card wins the round. (Aces are high in this game.) No one touches his card until the dealer says, "Indian." At that signal, each player picks up her card and, without peeking at it, holds it face out in front of her forehead. Players can see everyone's card but their own. Starting with the player to the left of the dealer, each player may place a bet with his or her counters, based on the facial expressions of the other players. Other players may "call" or "raise" any bet or "fold" (drop out of the round). When everyone has bet, players take their cards from their foreheads and look at them. After the winner has collected all the counters, the cards are collected, reshuffled, and dealt by the next dealer. To make the game easier, younger children can play with the number cards only.

# 70

# *Frog Jump*

**Objective:**

To move one set of frogs across their lily pads to the lily pads of another set of frogs, and vice versa, by jumping, or by sliding each frog to an empty pad.

**Players:**

1 or more

**Ages:**

7 and up

**Materials:**

writing materials; 3 dark and 3 light pebbles, poker chips, or other counters; chairs (for a group of 6 or more)

**Setting:**

inside or outside on the floor, at a table, or on a line of chairs

**Directions:**

For a game with fewer than 6 players, draw seven "lily pads" in a row across a paper (or in the dirt with a stick, or on the sidewalk with chalk). Place one light colored pebble, or chip, on each of the first three pads starting from the left, and one dark colored pebble on each of the last three pads, leaving the middle pad empty. This configuration represents a line of three light frogs on lily pads, an empty lily pad, and three dark frogs on lily pads. Players must move the light frogs to the lily pads of the dark frogs, and the dark frogs to the lily pads of the light frogs. This may only be done by jumping one frog over the other or by sliding to an empty lily pad. No backwards movements are allowed. Players may play individually by each creating a set of lily pads and frogs, or they may work in pairs or groups to solve the problem. In groups of 6 or more, the players themselves may become the frogs, using 7 chairs as the lily pads. They may try to solve the problem themselves or have other players command them to "jump" or "slide." Two or more individual players or teams may play to see who can complete the switch in the least number or moves. Other adaptations include changing the number of frogs/lily pads on either side by adding one or more, or be subtracting one, always keeping just one empty lily pad in the middle.

# 71

# *Palindromes*

**Objective:**

To take a number and add it to the reverse of itself, continuing the process with each sum until a sum is reached that reads the same in reverse as forward.

**Players:**

1 or more

**Ages:**

8 and up

**Materials:**

pencils and paper

**Setting:**

anywhere there is a writing surface

**Directions:**

Choose a number between 1 and 100. Then reverse the order of the digits and add the new number to the original number. Continue adding the reverses of each new sum until a palidrome is reached. *A palindrome is a number whose reverse is identical to the number itself, like 656 or 55.* For example, if a player selects a **29**, he adds the reverse, or **92**, to make **121**, a palindrome. Therefore, 29 is a one-step palindrome. Numbers from **1** to **9** are written with a zero in the tens place so that a reverse can easily be envisioned, like **07** whose reverse is **70**. Palindromes can always be reached, but sometimes the process takes several steps. The following are some examples. A player selects **39**. She adds its reverse: **39+93=132** (not a palindrome yet), adding again the reverse of the sum **132+231=363** (a palindrome); therefore **39** is a two-step palindrome. Another player selects **87**. Using the same procedure, here's how it would look: **87+78=165**; **165+651=726**; **726+627=1353**; **1353+3531=4884**. So **87** is a four-step palindrome. The high nineties are multi-step palindromes and can be a challenge for math wizards. Players may color code numbers by the number of steps it takes to reach a palindrome, then fill in the colors on a hundred's chart (a grid of 10 squares by 10 squares) to see patterns.

# 72

# *Odds or Evens*

**Objective:**
To guess whether hidden stones in a hand are of an odd or even number.

**Players:**
2 or more

**Ages:**
6 and up

**Materials:**
8 to 10 small stones, coins, or other small counters

**Setting:**
anywhere

**Directions:**
A player selected to be "It" holds pebbles in his hands and places them behind his back. He puts any amount into his right hand, closes it, and brings both hands forward. While he holds both hands out in front of him, the other players guess whether his right hand holds an "odd" number or "even" number. "It" also guesses. If "It" guesses correctly and other players guess correctly, "It" gets to have another turn until one player guesses correctly three times. If "It" guesses wrong and someone else guesses correctly, that person becomes "It." If everyone guesses incorrectly, the same "It" goes again. All players' scores return to zero each time a new player becomes "It."

# 73

# *Holding the Odds*

**Objective:**
To be the player with the odd-numbered counters at the end of the game.

**Players:**
2, or groups of 2

**Ages:**
7 and up

**Materials:**
an odd number of pebbles, beans, or other counters

**Setting:**
a flat surface indoors or outdoors

**Directions:**
Each pair of players sets out an odd number of counters in a cluster on a table or other flat surface. Players can take turns being first in each new round. Players take turns picking up one, two, or three counters. After all of the counters have been picked up, the player who has the odd number of counters is the winner of that round. Players may decide on how many rounds to play and keep a tally of their scores. The game may be changed to "Holding the Evens." Still using an odd number of counters, the player with the even number of counters is the winner.

# 74

# *Number Relay*

**Objective:**
  To run to a chalkboard and write down a number as fast as possible or to be the first to add up a series of numbers correctly.

**Players:**
  6 or more

**Ages:**
  6 and up

**Materials:**
  chalk and chalkboard or other writing materials

**Setting:**
  indoors, with space cleared for runners

**Directions:**
  Players divide into groups of 3 to 6. Groups of 3 or 4 are best for younger children. Someone divides a blackboard into spaces, one for each team, and sets a piece of chalk in front of each space. Both teams line up at the opposite end of the room from the blackboard behind starting lines. When a leader says, "Go," the first person from each team runs to her team's space at the blackboard, picks up a piece of chalk, and writes down a number. She runs back to her group and tags the hand of the next player, who runs to the board and writes another number directly below the first. This continues until the last player is tagged. That player runs to the board and adds up the numbers his teammates have written. The first team whose last player adds up his team's numbers correctly is the winner of the round. In successive rounds, players on each team rotate so that a different player is always the "adder." Older players may rule that the number must have two or three digits and/or that the digits must be higher than 4. Younger players may be limited to the use of single digit numbers.

# *SIDEWALK GAMES*

The games in this section have been selected because of their relative informality and the fact that few materials are needed to play them. They do not require large teams or special play areas. Two or more individuals can get together wherever there is a common sidewalk or hardtop surface and create a variety of games and other fun activities.

# 75

# Monster

**Objective:**

To toss a marker into designated spaces in order to draw all parts of a monster and crown it.

**Players:**

2 or more

**Ages:**

6 and up

**Materials:**

chalk; beanbag or flat stone; rags; pencils and paper (optional)

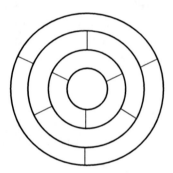

**Setting:**

a large sidewalk or hardtop area

**Directions:**

Draw a large circle on the cement or blacktop with chalk (about 4 to 5 feet across) and make three concentric circles within it. Divide all but the innermost circle into three even wedges. In each wedge, write one of these words: *arm, leg, nose, mouth, tail, ear, head, eye,* and *horn.* In the center circle, draw a crown. Before the game begins, each player draws the body of his or her monster with chalk on another part of the cement (or on paper with pencil). The players then decide how many of each part their monsters must have (for example, how many arms, eyes, and legs) before it is complete and may be "crowned."

As the game begins, the first player stands behind a throwing line, about three to four feet from the circles, and tosses the beanbag (or flat stone) into one of the spaces. Depending on where the beanbag lands, the player must draw that body part on his or her monster. Players must avoid throwing the beanbag into the center circle (the crown) until the monster has all of its parts. If the bag lands on the crown too soon, a player must erase a part of his or her monster. Players take one turn at a time until someone draws a complete monster and crowns it.

# 76

# *Giant Steps*

**Objective:**
To make one's way down the sidewalk to "Mother" by performing the kinds of steps Mother dictates.

**Players:**
4 or more

**Ages:**
5 and up

**Materials:**
none

**Setting:**
a long sidewalk or other outdoor area

**Directions:**
One player is selected as "Mother" and all other players line up about 50 feet down the sidewalk (playground, grass, etc.) from him. Mother calls the name of the first person and directs her to take steps, indicating what kind of steps and how many. Steps can include giant steps (long strides), baby steps (toe-to-heel steps), umbrella steps (step and spin once on one foot), duck steps (squat down and waddle), and backwards steps (walk backwards), and any other steps that the players decide upon. Each player must say, "Mother, may I?" before taking the steps or she loses her turn. "Mother" can also turn his back to the group, which allows the other players to sneak closer to him. However, if he turns around and sees anyone moving, the moving player must return to the starting line. The game continues this way until someone succeeds in tagging Mother and becomes the new "Mother" in the next round.

# Crazy 8's

**Objective:**

To count the number of tossed bottle caps that land within a drawn circle, and to be the first to reach the drawn square with that number written on it.

**Players:**

4 or more

**Ages:**

6 to 10

**Materials:**

8 bottlecaps (or flat stones), chalk

**Setting:**

a sidewalk or hardtop area

**Directions:**

With a piece of chalk, draw eight squares in a zig-zag pattern along a sidewalk or blacktop. Number the squares from 1 to 8 in a random pattern. At one end, draw a circle and a starting line. Players choose a leader, who tosses the bottle caps (or flat stones) in the air over the circle. As soon as the bottle caps land, the remaining players quickly count the number of caps that have landed in the circle and race for the square with that number written on it. The first to reach the correct square is the new leader.

125

# *Train Tracks*

**Objective:**

To be the first to knock over a can with a ball from 5 different distances.

**Payers:**

2 or more

**Ages:**

8 and up

**Materials:**

aluminum soda pop can, sand or dirt, two tennis balls, chalk

**Setting:**

a sidewalk or hardtop area

**Directions:**

With chalk, draw 5 (or more) "train tracks" along a sidewalk about three large steps apart. Write a number on each track. Place an inch or so of sand in the bottom of a soft drink can or plastic soft drink bottle and set it about 6 steps from track 1. Players take turns throwing the tennis balls at the can starting on track 5 (or the largest numbered track). Each player gets two tries to hit the can during each turn. If a player hits the can, she may then move up one track and continue her turn until she misses both tries from one track. The game ends when a player hits the can from track 1.

# 79

# *Chinese Hopscotch*

**Objective:**
To take turns hopping through a maze of sticks, relay fashion,
picking up one stick with each turn, until all of the sticks are gone.

**Players:**
8 or more

**Ages:**
6 and up

**Materials:**
popsicle sticks, used chopsticks, or any other lightweight sticks.

**Setting:**
a sidewalk

**Directions:**
Players divide into two teams. Each team lines up a row of sticks
along one side of a sidewalk, perpendicular to the edge. Sticks are
placed evenly about 18 inches apart, or far enough apart to allow
players to make one hop over each. Both teams line up behind their
first stick. When someone shouts, "Go!," the first person in each
line hops over each stick until he comes to the end stick, which he
picks up. He turns around on the same foot and hops back over the
remaining sticks. When he reaches his team, he tags the next in
line who hops over the sticks, picks up the last one, and hops back.
Each player goes to the end of the line after having a turn (in case
there are more sticks than people). Any player who puts down a
foot or steps on a stick while hopping must go back to the beginning
and start her turn again.

# 80

# *Hopscotch*

**Objective:**
To toss a flat object into a series of shapes drawn on the sidewalk, and to hop through the shapes which contain no objects.

**Players:**
2 or more

**Ages:**
7 and up

**Materials:**
chalk; flat pebbles, bottlecaps, or heavy coins

**Setting:**
a sidewalk

**Directions:**
Draw a hopscotch design on the sidewalk with chalk. An easy diagram can be made by using four sidewalk "squares." Divide one square into four equal squares using perpendicular lines. Split the next square into four triangles with crossed lines drawn from corner to corner. Divide the third square so that it is identical to the first. In the fourth square, draw a semicircle facing the hopscotch diagram and label it "Free." Write a number in each space, beginning with "1" in the first left-hand square and continuing in order up to 12.

To begin the game, the first player must toss a flat object, called a potsie, into space 1. If it lands in the space, he hops through the diagram, on one foot for single spaces, two feet for side-by-side spaces. When he reaches the "free" space, he can rest on two feet, turn around and hop back until he reaches the box which contains

his potsie. He bends over, picks up the potsie, and jumps out of the diagram.  He continues by throwing his potsie into space 2, and hopping through the diagram again.  A player loses her turn if her potsie does not fall into the space intended.  The potsie is then put back in the last space played while the next player takes a turn.  Other grounds for losing a turn are putting two feet in one space, jumping into any space containing a potsie, or touching a hopscotch line with hands or feet while playing.  Players attempt to work their way through all of the spaces.  The game is best played with a limit of four players per hopscotch diagram.

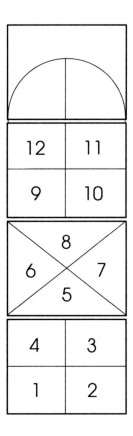

# 81

# *Tightrope Walking*

**Objective:**
To walk down a straight line, heel-to-toe fashion, and perform one stunt halfway down the line.

**Players:**
1 or more

**Ages:**
7 and up

**Materials:**
chalk and yardstick or two 15-foot lengths of string

**Setting:**
a sidewalk or other open area with a hard surface

**Directions:**
With chalk and a yardstick, draw two parallel lines down the sidewalk about 15 feet long and 2 to 3 feet apart. For one to three players, a single line down the middle will suffice. String may be used in place of the chalk lines if it is held in place at both ends by rocks or other heavy objects.

Each player takes a turn "walking the tightrope" by stepping onto the line with one foot and placing the heel of the other foot directly in front of the first foot. To add to the fun, players may use a broomstick as a balance pole. When a player has made it to the middle of the line, she must perform some kind of special move, like extending a leg behind her and leaning forward, turning around, jumping three times, or any other creative "high wire" movement.

Of course, if a player "falls off" the tightrope, he must give up his turn and go to the end of the line. Four or more players can have a race down two parallel lines, using the same moves. If a player falls off, she must go back to the beginning and start over again. The game can be varied by drawing a line with curves and loops.

# Red Light, Green Light

**Objective:**
To reach and tag the "traffic light" by running without being caught.

**Players:**
4 or more

**Ages:**
5 and up

**Materials:**
none

**Setting:**
a sidewalk or other open area

**Directions:**
One player is selected to be the "traffic light." The other players line up about 25 feet away from her. The traffic light begins the game by turning her back to the players while calling out, "Green light!" While her back is turned, the other players move towards her as quickly as they can. After a few seconds, she calls out again, saying, "One-two-three, Red light!" At the words "Red light," she snaps around to face the other players. The players must "freeze" before she sees them. If the "traffic light" sees any player move, she calls out his name and he must return to the starting line. The "traffic light" turns around again and the game continues in the same manner until one player tags the "traffic light" without being caught. That player becomes the new "traffic light."

# 83

# *Straw Race*

**Objective:**
To blow a wad of paper along a sidewalk joint to a midline, using a straw.

**Players:**
2 or more

**Ages:**
6 and up

**Materials:**
one drinking straw per player, chalk, small bits of paper

**Setting:**
along a joint of a sidewalk

**Directions:**
With a piece of chalk, a player draws a line across a sidewalk joint midway between the two sides of the sidewalk. The first two players each wad a small piece of paper into a tight ball. Next they set their paperwad in the groove at opposite ends of the sidewalk joint, about an inch from the sidewalk edge. A third player kneels in the middle and acts as judge. When the judge says, "Take your positions," players kneel on the ground, facing each other on the sidewalk edges. At "Go," the players blow through their straws, forcing their paperwads to move down the "track" to the finish line. If a paperwad gets blown off track, it must be blown back on. Players attempt to be the first person to reach the line, and may play individually or in teams for points.

# TAG GAMES

The "chase" has been a human theme since time immemorial. Early hunters chased the animals that provided them with food and clothing. Children have always raced to and from school and in parks and playgrounds. They have invented countless variations of this simple activity that, in most instances, require nothing but a set of rules and a pair of legs.

This section features tag games to be played for the fun of chasing, running, and even getting caught. Whoever is "It" becomes the focus of everyone's attention, and the runners too receive attention, one at a time.

# Streets and Alleys

**Objective:**

To assume the position of "streets," "alleys," and "lampposts" with other players; to chase and tag someone if you are "It;" to escape from being tagged if you are being chased.

**Players:**

11 or more

**Ages:**

8 and up

**Materials:**

**Setting:**

a open area outdoors or indoors

**Directions:**

One player is selected to be the "chaser" and another, the "runner." The rest of the players line up in rows of equal number to form a matrix. For example, if there are 16 players, not including the chaser and the runner, they line up in four rows of four, each an arm's length from the player on either side and the players in front and behind. All players face the same direction and practice the three positions before the game starts. When a designated "caller" yells, "Streets," all players hold their arms straight out to the sides. When "Alleys," is called, players make a quarter turn to the right so that they are facing the back of the person who was on their right. Arms are still extended. To return to the "Streets" position, everyone turns a quarter turn back to their left. To assume the "Lampposts" position, players stand straight with their hands at their sides.

The chaser tries to tag the runner within the maze of players. The runner and chaser start out at opposite ends of the configuration, and the players begin in the "Lampposts" position. Within seconds, the caller shouts a different command and the players take that position. The chaser and runner may not break through the arms of other players to run or tag. Therefore, they must stay within the rows and columns created by the "Streets" and "Alleys" commands. Only the "Lampposts" position gives them the freedom to move in all directions. If the runner is tagged, she becomes the new chaser and a new runner is chosen. The game can be varied by allowing the runner to tap any player on the shoulder and change places with him or her. This creates a more involving, fast changing game.

# 85

# *Dragon Tag*

**Objective:**

To make a player part of the "dragon" by surrounding him with a line of players; to escape being surrounded by the dragon.

**Players:**

10 minimum

**Ages:**

7 and up

**Materials:**

**Setting:**

outdoors

**Directions:**

Four to five players join hands to become the "dragon." The dragon runs around trying to form a circle around one or more other players. As soon as a player is surrounded by the dragon, he or she must become a part of the dragon by joining hands at one end of the line. As the game proceeds, the dragon gets longer. If any player who is part of the dragon breaks hands, the whole dragon must stop until hands are rejoined. The game ends when all of the players are captured and have become part of the dragon.

# 86

# *Crows and Cranes*

**Objective:**

To tag a player from the other team, making that person join your team; to avoid being tagged by a member of the opposite team.

**Players:**

10 or more

**Ages:**

6 and up

**Materials:**

**Setting:**

a large outdoor space

**Directions:**

One player is selected as a "caller." The rest of the players are divided into two teams, the Crows and the Cranes. Each team draws a goal line about 100 feet from the other team and stands behind it, facing the other team. The caller stands in the middle and calls, "Start walking!" The teams must begin walking toward each other. As they walk closer to each other, the caller shouts out the name of one of the teams. He begins by exaggerating and holding the sound, "Cr-r-r-r-r...," and finishes with one of the team names. Whichever team he names must turn around and run for its goal line. The other team chases the running players and tries to tag them before they reach the safety of their goal line. Any players tagged must join the opposing team. Both teams line up again for the next round. The game ends at the close of a pre-established time period, with one team having all or most of the players.

# 87

# *Catch the Dragon's Tail*

**Objective:**
For the dragon's head to catch its own tail or the tail of another dragon.

**Players:**
8 or more

**Ages:**
6 and up

**Materials:**
none

**Setting:**
a large outdoor area

**Directions:**
If you have fewer than 14 players, play this game by making one "dragon." Players line up with hands on the shoulders or waist of the person in front of them. The first person is named the "head" of the dragon and the last person is the dragon's "tail." The head tries to catch the tail by running around in a zig-zag pattern or circle. The tail tries to avoid being caught by the head. The rest of the dragon must hold on tightly and move as effectively as it can. If the head catches the tail, it becomes the tail and the next player in line becomes the head.

If the group is large, players form 2 or more dragons. In this game, a dragon's head tries to catch the tail of another dragon without having its own tail caught! If the tail of a dragon is caught, the dragon is "out." The game ends when one dragon is left. A new game can begin with the same dragons, but with a different head and tail.

# Blind Man's Bluff

**Objective:**
To catch and identify a player while blindfolded; to avoid being caught by the blind player.

**Players:**
8 or more

**Ages:**
5 and up

**Materials:**
blindfold

**Setting:**
an open area outdoors or indoors

**Directions:**
One player volunteers, or is selected, to be the blind player. He puts a blindfold around his eyes and stands in the center of the other players who form a circle around him. The players join hands and walk or skip to a song or chant. When the blind player calls, "Stop," the circled players stop moving and singing. The blind player points to a spot in the circle, and the person nearest that spot drops hands with the players on either side of her and steps into the circle. She makes a noise with her feet to indicate that she has entered the circle. Then the blind player tries to catch her. She ducks and moves around inside the circle. The other players have rejoined hands so that the blind player does not stray from the circle. Sooner or later the blind player catches the other player. Then he must try to identify her by touching her head and face only. If he identifies her, she becomes the next blind player. If he does not correctly name her, he must try again during the next round.

# 89

# *Hug Tag*

**Objective:**
To tag someone "out" or to avoid being tagged by hugging a partner.

**Players:**
as many as possible, but at least 10

**Ages:**
6 and up

**Materials:**
none

**Setting:**
outdoors

**Directions:**
This is much like the traditional tag game in that one person volunteers or is selected to be "It." "It" tries to tag people out. Instead of a "base" or free area, however, players are safe only when they are hugging another person. Anyone tagged by "It" must then become "It." After playing for a while, change the rule so that three people must be hugging to be safe from being tagged, then four. If players won't move from the safety of their hugs, a rule can be added whereby they must disengage while "It" stands still and counts to ten. The game can also be varied by having players who are tagged join "It" in tagging others until everyone is tagged.

# *WORD GAMES*

Most word games require few or no materials and can be played
while traveling in a car, waiting at a doctor's office, walking to
school, or just about anywhere two or more willing players come
together.

Word games enlarge vocabularies, enhance word knowledge
and usage, and encourage players to think creatively. The more
frequently players engage in word games, the more proficient they
become in the use of verbal skills.

# 90

# *Coffeepot*

**Objective:**
To guess the name of an activity by asking, "yes" and "no" questions.

**Players:**
2 or more

**Ages:**
8 and up

**Materials:**
none

**Setting:**
anywhere

**Directions:**
One player is designated the "Questioner" and is asked to move out of earshot of the other players by going to a far corner of the room or leaving the room. The remaining players identify an activity that can be performed by a person or animal, such as driving a car, playing tennis, climbing a tree, or swimming in the ocean. From that point on, the chosen activity is referred to as, "coffeepot." When the absent player is called back, he or she is directed to ask questions in order to determine what "coffeepotting" is. Questions must be answerable with a "yes" or "no" response. Players either agree on a time limit for the questioning or limit the number of questions asked. At any time during the questioning period, the Questioner may guess the identity of coffeepot. If the guess is correct, another person may have a turn. If the Questioner misses three guesses, he or she is "out" and must let another person have a turn.

# 91

# *Hang Man*

**Objective:**

To recognize a word based on the number of letters in the word and by identifying as few of the word's actual letters as possible.

**Players:**

3 or more

**Ages:**

7 or 8 and up

**Materials:**

chalk and chalkboard or other writing materials

**Setting:**

indoors or outdoors

**Directions:**

A leader thinks of a word and, on chalkboard or paper, draws as many side-by-side horizontal lines as there are letters in the word. Then the leader draws a gallows, which looks like a large 7. The other players each take turns guessing the letters in the word. If a guess is correct, the letter is written on the line that corresponds to its location in the word. If the first guess is wrong, the leader draws a head under the top of the gallows. Each wrong guess adds another body part, until head, body, two arms, two legs (and two feet and two hands, if the word is long or difficult) have been drawn. With the last wrong guess, the leader draws a noose around the head which "hangs" the figure, ending the game. A new game begins with the leader choosing another word. If the word is guessed before the figure is hanged, the group wins. The person who guesses the word or names the last correct letter becomes the leader of the new game.

# *Outa This World*

**Objective:**
To guess a category by learning which words are within and which words are outside of the category.

**Players:**
3 or more

**Ages:**
8 and up

**Materials:**
chalk and chalkboard or other writing materials

**Setting:**
indoors or outdoors

**Directions:**
A leader draws a large circle on a chalkboard (or paper) and thinks of any category into which objects or other things can be classified. Examples are "motorized vehicles," "things to write with," "animals with four feet," "trees," "occupations," "musical instruments," and so on. The other players try to guess the category by first naming words which could fit *any* category. If a word fits the secret category, the leader writes it inside the circle and says, "It's in this world." If a word does not fit the category, the leader writes it outside the circle and says, "It's outa this world." For example, if the category were motorized vehicles, the word *lamp* would be written outside the circle, but the word *truck* would be inside the circle. The game continues until the group guesses the category. The person who guesses the category or contributes the last word becomes the leader of the next game.

# 93

# *Hinky Pinky*

**Objective:**
To make up a two-word rhyme and define it; to guess a two-word rhyme upon hearing its definition.

**Players:**
2 or more

**Ages:**
7 and up

**Materials:**
none

**Setting:**
anywhere

**Directions:**
One player thinks of two rhyming words that have the same number of syllables and that, together, have some kind of meaning. For example, he may think of the words *big pig*. Next, the same player thinks of a definition of the two words (or a way to describe them), such as "a large hog." He begins the game by indicating to the other players how many syllables make up each word in the pair. He calls it a "Hink Pink" if the words are single syllable words like "big pig;" a "Hinky Pinky" if they are double syllable words such as "rattle battle;" or a "Hinkety Pinkety" if they are triple syllable words like "induction production." Older players may be challenged by four syllable words, such as "Mendicino palomino." These are referred to as "Hinkeronis Pinkeronis." Next, the player describes or defines the word pair. Finally, the other players guess the rhyming words. The person who guesses may be the next to think of a rhyming pair, or players may take turns.

# 94

# *First and Last*

**Objective:**
To name an object in a given category that begins with the last letter of the previous word named in that category.

**Players:**
2 or more

**Ages:**
8 and up

**Materials:**
none

**Setting:**
anywhere

**Directions:**
Players decide on a category, such as Food. The first player begins by naming any object in that category. The second player must name an object whose first letter is the same as the last letter of the first object named. The third player must name an object beginning with the last letter of the second player's word. No words may be repeated. The game ends when none of the players can think of a word with the required first letter. Then another category is selected and the game begins again.

# 95

# *Connections*

**Objective:**

To explain how two unrelated words can be connected.

**Players:**

2 or more

**Ages:**

8 and up

**Materials:**

**Setting:**

anywhere

**Directions:**

Player #1 names a word. Player #2 names a word which seems unrelated to the first. Player #1 must then think of a way in which the two words can be related and explain the relationship. For example, Player #1 says "pork chop." Player #2 says "computer." Player #1 might make a connection between the two by saying, "A pork chop comes from a pig raised on a farm. The farmer uses a computer to keep track of the prices he gets for his pigs each year. Both are important to the farmer." Then Player #2 says a word, Player #3 names a seemingly unrelated word, and Player #2 must think of a way to create a relationship between the two words. The game moves to one new player each time a new round is played. The last player may partner with player number one.

# 96

# *Telegrams*

**Objective:**

To create a telegram, beginning each word in the telegram with a letter prescribed in advance by the group.

**Players:**

2 or more

**Ages:**

8 and up

**Materials:**

pencils and paper

**Setting:**

any space that has writing surfaces

**Directions:**

In this game, individual players create a telegram, beginning each word in the telegram with a letter prescribed in advance by the group. First, players decide how many words their telegrams will contain. A good basic range is 5 to 12 words, with as many as 15 words for older players. One player chooses the first letter of the first word. Everyone writes that letter down on paper, leaving a space for the remainder of the word. A second player chooses the first letter of the second word, and the players record it, again leaving a space for the remainder of the word. Players take turns choosing the first letters of the remaining words. Each player must then create a telegram using words which begin with the chosen letters in the order they were selected. If the group chooses the letters B, T, S, L, O, and Z, the telegram might read, "Big time

spender leaves our zoo," or "Better to silently leave our zone."
A time limit of 5 minutes (more or less) may be agreed upon by
the group. The rules may be adapted to make the game easier for
younger players. For example, younger players may be allowed to
work in pairs or small teams or to rearrange the order of the letters.

# 97

# *Adverbs*

**Objective:**
To carry out a command in the mood of an assigned adverb.

**Players:**
2 or more

**Ages:**
9 and up

**Materials:**
none

**Setting:**
anywhere

**Directions:**
When this game is played by two players, one thinks up the adverb and does the acting and the other is the Guesser. In groups of three or more, one player is selected to be the Guesser. The Guesser leaves the room (or goes out of earshot) while the other players decide on an adverb. Some easy adverbs are, "quickly," "loudly," "happily," or "gently." Harder ones might be "creatively," "lavishly," "moderately," "vigorously," or "prayerfully." When the players have decided on the adverb, they call the Guesser back to the group. The Guesser then asks individual members of the group to perform an action in the manner described by the adverb. For example, the guesser might say, "Tania, walk across the room in the manner of the adverb," or "Julio, say 'Hello,' to Lucinda in the manner of the adverb. The designated person performs the action in the fashion that the adverb describes. Players may decide at the start of the game how many commands and guesses the Guesser can make before the adverb is revealed. The last person to act out an adverb that is guessed correctly becomes the next Guesser.

# 98

# *Taboo*

**Objective:**
To answer a question in such a way that a "taboo" letter is not contained in the answer.

**Players:**
2 or more

**Ages:**
9 and up

**Materials:**
none

**Setting:**
anywhere

**Directions:**
One player is chosen to be the leader. That player selects a letter which is labeled "taboo." None of the other players may speak a word that contains the taboo letter. The game begins with the leader asking the first player a question that requires more than a one-word answer. For example, the leader may ask, "What is your favorite football team and why?" The player must answer the question without using the taboo letter. If the taboo letter is "R," the player might answer, "The team that means Indians because I lived in that city for a long time." The player has answered the question without using the "R" in "Redskins" by substituting other words that still make sense. The leader asks each player a different question. Any player who speaks a word containing the taboo letter must drop out of the game. The last remaining person becomes the leader of a new game. If more than 10 people are playing, they may divide into two teams. The leaders of the two teams take turns asking questions of individual members of the opposite team. The game is played until all the players on one team are out.

# 99

# *No, You Mean...*

**Objective:**
To find rhyming or similar-sounding words and describe them.

**Players:**
2 or more

**Ages:**
9 and up

**Materials:**
none

**Setting:**
anywhere

**Directions:**
The first player chooses a word, one which has rhyming or similar sounding words, such as *stick*. The person uses the word in a sentence in place of a rhyming word that would make sense in the sentence. For example, the player might say, "I want to play a 'stick' on my brother." The second player must say, "No, you mean 'trick,'" and then describe a different rhyming word like, "a tiny insect that sucks the blood of larger animals." The third player might say, "No, you mean, 'tick,' to hit someone with a foot," and the fourth player might continue, "No, you mean kick, a hard, rectangular stone that is usually red," and so on. The object is to keep the words rhyming and changing from player to player. Similar sounding words can also be used, such as *weather* and *wetter*, thus changing the sound to be rhymed. Players must agree that the words sound similar enough before the game may proceed. The last player who successfully describes a new rhyming word gets to start the next round.

# 100

# *Parts of Speech*

**Objective:**
To create a group sentence by naming a word representing an assigned part of speech.

**Players:**
4 or more

**Ages:**
9 and up

**Materials:**
optional 3" x 5" cards and pencils

**Setting:**
anywhere

**Directions:**
Players divide into groups of four to six. Each player is assigned one of the following parts of speech: *noun, verb, adjective,* and *adverb* (for four players). With a fifth player, add *prepositional phrase*; with a sixth player, add a *second* adjective or prepositional phrase. The players silently think of a word representing their assigned part of speech. Then, one player at a time reveals his or her chosen word. The players arrange the words so that they create a sentence, no matter how silly it sounds. If more than one team is playing the game, have the teams share their sentences by lining up in the same order as the order of words in their sentence, and having members call out their word. All players may decide which sentence is the funniest. A team of four may create a sentence that says, "Wet eyeballs smell quickly." A team of five may come up with a sentence like, "Green monkeys feverishly crash after the storm." Teams may also write their words on cards so that they can arrange and rearrange them to "see" as well as hear different sentences.

If your heart is in Social-Emotional
Learning, visit us online.

Come see us at
www.InnerchoicePublishing.com

Our web site gives you a look at all our other Social-Emotional
Learning-based books, free activities, articles, research, and
learning and teaching strategies. Every week you'll get a new
Sharing Circle topic and lesson.

INNERCHOICE Publishing
15079 Oak Chase Court
Wellington, FL 33414

CPSIA information can be obtained at www.ICGtesting.com
Printed in the USA
BVOW04s1930231013

334500BV00010BA/252/P